SPECIAL BREW

AN INSIDE LOOK AT THE
2018 MILWAUKEE BREWERS

SPECIAL BREW

AN INSIDE LOOK AT THE 2018 MILWAUKEE BREWERS

BY **TOM HAUDRICOURT**

KCI *SPORTS PUBLISHING*

ISBN: 1-940056-75-3
ISBN 13: 978-1-940056-75-3

Printed in the United States of America.
KCI Sports Publishing 3340 Whiting Avenue, Suite 5
Stevens Point, WI 54481
Phone: 1-800-697-3756 Fax: 715-344-2668
www.kcisports.com

Photos courtesy of: AP Images

Book Layout and Design: Nicky Brillowski

DEDICATION

Every time I write a book, I'm amazed that I've done it. I'm always grateful that my wife, Trish, understands what it means to me to undertake such a project and provides her complete support. And apologies to Digger and Dexter, our second duo of dachshunds, for not being available to play as often in doing so. Find a toy and let's go.

ACKNOWLEDGMENTS

I have covered the Milwaukee Brewers since August 1985, except for a brief period in 2002-'03 when I covered the New York Yankees for the Bergen (N.J.) Record. It took me quite a while to chronicle my first playoff team, with the Brewers and CC Sabathia breaking through in 2008 to win what then was the only National League wild card berth.

The Brewers have returned to October baseball twice since that season, under different circumstances. The 2011 Brewers, under new manager Ron Roenicke, figured to be good and were even better, claiming their first NL Central crown. I thought that team had a good chance to go to the World Series but the St. Louis Cardinals, long a thorn in Milwaukee's side, had other ideas, knocking off the Brewers in six games in the NLCS.

The 2014 Brewers appeared headed back to the postseason before suffering a massive collapse over the last six weeks. As it turned out, that slide was not a fluke. The '15 club staggered out of the gate, Roenicke was fired, and a large-scale rebuilding process began. Craig Counsell was tabbed as the new manager, which proved to be a brilliant move. General manager Doug Melvin later stepped aside in favor of 30-year-old David Stearns, who joined the growing legion of young Ivy Leaguers running clubs throughout the majors.

Nobody knew what would happen next, or how long it might take. But Stearns and his staff made many genius personnel moves, and Counsell held the team together on the field under the theme "stay connected." When the '17 club took an unexpected leap forward, missing the playoffs by one game, principal owner Mark Attanasio and Stearns decided to move from rebuild to go-for-it mode.

The rest is history, as they say. The 2018 Brewers caught fire at exactly the right time, reeling off eight victories in a row to end the season, then four more in the playoffs. And George Webb cooked up some free burgers. Included in that incredible run was the Game No. 163 showdown in Wrigley Field, when the runaway Brewers wrested the division crown from the Cubs in dramatic fashion.

This book is more than a recap of those events. It's an inside look at the decisions, the decision makers and the players who made it all happen, some who were expected to excel, others who seemingly came out of the blue. Being there on a daily basis as a beat writer for the Milwaukee Journal Sentinel, I had a close-up look at the inner workings of this remarkable season. My goal with this book was to peel the curtain back a bit and give readers that inside, in-depth analysis of how this close-knit, fun-loving bunch gave their fans one heck of a ride, particularly over the final couple of months.

The quotes and game details in the book came from coverage in the Journal Sentinel, either by myself or fellow beat writer Todd Rosiak. Todd joined me on the beat in 2011, so he has covered two division titles by the Brewers. I constantly remind him that I had to wait nearly 23 years for my first playoff team, and he tells me that's my problem, not his. And he is right. Water under the dam. Todd gets my thanks for listening to me re-tell the same stories and jokes, day after day, and make old-guy references he doesn't quite understand, with only minor complaints.

I am fortunate at this late stage of my career to have chronicled such a memorable season by the Brewers, and grateful to Stearns and Counsell for having the patience to answer my constant questions while also trusting me with background information to make sure I knew of what I wrote. I also thank the team's always helpful media relations department and the many other staff members who work hard on a daily basis. The Brewers are a pleasure to cover because they are, first of all, nice people.

I also want to thank the folks at KCI Sports Publishing for the willingness to collaborate with me on a book for the second time. Peter Clark and his staff are the kind of people with whom writers enjoy working.

So, here we go. I hope you enjoy reading this book as much as I enjoyed writing it. Carry on.

.

CONTENTS

CHRISTIAN YELICH
2018 NATIONAL LEAGUE MVP

The 2018 season was truly a remarkable journey. It started in spring training, getting to know everybody, in my case. I had to learn new teammates, a new organization, a new city. You're going into it with an open mind, but you don't really know what to expect. There's no guarantee it goes well or that it will be a smooth transition. Fortunately for me, it was. And it ended up being a magical year. So much happened over the course of the season, it's difficult to remember it all. The chemistry we had in the clubhouse is unique to most teams. It's not the same on every team, and it's not always like that every year. We weren't just teammates. We were friends. We enjoyed hanging out together. Those bonds are important because when you're playing those big games in hostile stadiums, it's a cool feeling to know your teammates have your back. It's a great feeling to succeed like that with your friends.

Our goal was always to win the division. People were saying if we were going to make the playoffs it had to be through the Wild Card, but we never thought that, not as long as we were still alive. We weren't going to quit on that goal of the division title until we were eliminated. That's why we had to focus on every game. We couldn't get caught up looking ahead. We had to win that night's game, then focus on the next one. That's how we got to eight wins in a row at the end of the season. Our mentality was to concentrate on the 'now,' and that's why we ended up being so successful. The final stretch of the season was so crazy. It was so loud

when we played Detroit in our final home series at Miller Park. For me, personally, the "MVP!" chants were truly amazing. I never expected anything like that. I can't even remember at what point of the season it began, but it was incredible. We had so much at stake down the stretch, and the fans really helped us by creating such a loud environment. There were so many crazy things going on that made all of it so special. You never expect to win an MVP Award. It's really hard to describe what that feels like when you get that news. As both a player and a team, it's really cool. It's one of those awards that's truly special. I had such tremendous support from my teammates and the fans. In my mind, what made winning the MVP even better was the success we had as a team. That's what made it all so enjoyable. I just wanted to help our team win. I give credit to everyone – players, coaches, staff – for making it easy on me. One of my favorite memories for the whole year was Game No. 163 at Wrigley Field. No one thought we had a chance to go in there and win the division. Once we got to that game, we all knew we could do it. Winning that game sums up the whole year. It's probably the most fun I've ever had. It meant so much to everybody – the team, our fans, the city. It's something you never forget.

For me and many of my teammates, the 2018 season is one that won't soon be forgotten. Hopefully, we can take it one step further in 2019. I know the Brewers fans will be with us the whole way.

So, once again, let's gooooooo!

ALLAN H. "BUD" SELIG

Tom Haudricourt's wonderful book about the 2018 Milwaukee Brewers and their improbable run deep into the Major League Baseball post-season is in many respects a love story between a city and its baseball team. No matter where in Milwaukee and Wisconsin one was during the months of September and October, people were talking about the Brewers and baseball.

The buzz really began to hit a fever pitch in mid-September, when out of nowhere, what seemed like the impossible dream for the Brewers began to look and feel, incredibly, like it might actually happen. All of a sudden, the team's loyal fans, who had watched somewhat anxiously all season, began pumping their fists and chanting for the Brewers.

Wherever I went in the city during that time, I was stopped by fans wearing all sorts of Brewers gear who asked me if the team could overtake the Cubs and make it to the post-season. Even my wife, Sue, would wear a Christian Yelich jersey to support the team and her new favorite player.

For me, it brought back the great excitement of years past. It was like 1982 all over again, the season the Brewers beat the California Angels in the American League Championship Series before losing the World Series in seven agonizing games to the St. Louis Cardinals. It also brought back wonderful memories of 1957 and 1958 when the Milwaukee Braves first beat the New York Yankees in the World Series and then lost the following year. That's how charged the atmosphere was in the city as the Brewers closed in on the Cubs.

Incredibly, the Brewers won their final eight games of the regular season, including the tie-breaking victory

over the Cubs in Game No. 163 to clinch the National
League Central, then beat the Colorado Rockies three
straight to win the NL Division Series. Next, they
beat the Los Angeles Dodgers in Game 1 of the NL
Championship Series to run their win streak to an even
dozen games, an incredible feat at that time of year.
But, sadly, all good things must come to an end. It was
tough to take but the Dodgers beat the Brewers in seven
games, getting stretched to the limit.

For the first time in many years, I could unabashedly
root for my hometown team. As Commissioner of
Baseball, it was my job to remain as unbiased as
possible, not an easy task considering my longtime
ties to the Brewers. While it was a heart-breaking loss,
it was a great moment in Milwaukee and Wisconsin
baseball history that none of us ever will forget. This
book gives us an inside look at that wonderful time.

CHAPTER ONE

January 25, 2018

It was the day the Milwaukee Brewers' rebuilding process moved into high gear.

January 25, 2018.

That was the day the Brewers acquired outfielders Christian Yelich and Lorenzo Cain within hours of each other, the first via trade with the Miami Marlins and the latter with a five-year, $80-million deal, the largest free-agent signing in franchise history. The expectation of general manager David Stearns was that Yelich and Cain would transform a swing-and-miss, power-dependent offense that ran hot and cold in 2017, when the Brewers fell one victory short of tying for the second wild-card berth in the National League.

Yelich and Cain would greatly exceed that expectation, sparking the Brewers within one game of their first World Series berth since 1982. With a second half for the ages, Yelich would run away with the NL MVP award, blowing past Chicago Cubs infielder Javy Baez, the acknowledged favorite entering the final month of the season.

Difficult as it might be to believe, Stearns had no idea the dual pursuits of Yelich and Cain would cross the finish line almost simultaneously. He had been negotiating for many weeks with Cain's agent, Damon Lapa, after being told in the early going that the multi-talented center fielder had keen interest in returning to Milwaukee, the team that originally drafted him before sending him to Kansas City in December 2010 in the blockbuster trade for pitching ace Zack Greinke.

Cain blossomed during his time with the Royals, becoming a key component of an upstart club that fell just short of winning the 2014 World Series, losing in seven games to Madison Bumgarner and the San Francisco Giants, before bouncing back the next season to overwhelm the New York Mets and claim its first championship since 1985.

Stearns figured Cain would have a many-layered effect on the Brewers. He batted mostly in the third spot in the order for Kansas City but Stearns and manager Craig Counsell envisioned Cain as a top of the order force who would get on base and set the table for the middle of the lineup. Cain had established himself as one of the top defenders at his position, a fearless, instinctive center fielder who chased down balls in the gaps with remarkable closing speed and snatched away home runs with spectacular leaps against the wall.

The free-agent market was moving at the speed of a glacier, signaling a new era of cautious spending by clubs now being run by Ivy League brainiacs. But Lapa insisted on a five-year deal, something that caused pause by some suitors, with Cain due to turn 32 a week into the 2018 season.

Modern analytics have not been kind to players in their 30s, who often struggle with drops in production or injuries, if not both. The Brewers had first-hand experience in that department with left fielder Ryan Braun, who was missing more and more time in recent seasons with nagging injuries, particularly to his back, legs and right thumb.

A five-year deal would take Cain beyond his mid 30s, giving Stearns and his staff much to deliberate within the inner sanctum of Miller Park. But, after careful study and consideration, the Brewers' brain trust decided that if any player would be an exception to the aging rule, it was Cain, who didn't start playing baseball until his senior year in high school.

"In his early 30s, he is becoming a better player than he was in his late 20s," reasoned Stearns.

The numbers supported that argument. In 2015, at age 29, Cain had produced his best season, batting .307 with 16 home runs, 72 RBI, .838 OPS and 28 stolen bases, earning his first All-Star berth. His production waned the next season, in large part due to an ailing wrist that limited him to 103 games.

But Cain bounced back in impressive fashion in 2017, batting .300 with a .363 OBP, 15 homers, 49 RBI and 26 steals while playing in a career-high 155 games.

Lapa explained to Stearns the lengths with which Cain had gone to protect his health and make his body stronger. The Florida native had been training for several years at the University of Oklahoma, and he now was powerfully built at 6-2, 205 pounds.

Outfielder Chuckie Caufield, a teammate at the Brewers' Class A Brevard County, Fla., affiliate in 2008, had attended OU and invited Cain to train with him there in the off-season. Cain's trips to Norman, Okla., became more frequent after he met Sooners gymnast Jenny Baker. A romance soon blossomed and they later married. Cain eventually moved to Norman full time to continue training under well-respected strength and conditioning coach Tim Overman.

Stearns knew an $80 million investment in one player was nothing to take lightly while running a small-market team that played for two seasons with a $60

The Brewers rebuild went into high-speed when GM David Stearns signed Christian Yelich and Lorenzo Cain on January 25, 2018.
AP PHOTO

million payroll after stripping the roster of veterans
with big salaries. But owner Mark Attanasio trusted the
young GM – he had been hired at the tender age of 30
in 2015 – to know what he was doing and committed to
spending the most money any free-agent position player
would make that winter.

The pursuit of Yelich was a completely different
animal. New management, under the direction of former
New York Yankees icon Derek Jeter, was holding a fire
sale in Miami, where high spending and low attendance
had wreaked havoc with team finances. Slugger
extraordinaire Giancarlo Stanton was dealt to the New
York Yankees, speedy second baseman Dee Gordon to
Seattle and outfielder Marcel Ozuna to St. Louis.

Yelich had signed a seven-year, $49.57 million
contract extension, with a club option, after his first full
season with the Marlins in 2014, figuring the talent-
laden team was heading for bigger and better things.
But young pitching star Jose Fernandez was killed in
the final week of the 2016 season in a tragic boating
accident, the team was sold and cost-cutting became the
order of the day.

An unhappy Yelich told his agent, Joe Longo, to ask
to also be traded. Longo went a step further, doing an
interview with a national sports outlet and proclaiming
the relationship between team and player was
"irretrievably broken."

"They have a plan," Longo said. "I respect that plan,
but that plan shouldn't include Christian at this point in
his career. Christian's in the middle of the best years of
his career, and having him be part of a 100-loss season
is not really where we want to see him going."

That declaration certainly didn't help the bargaining
position of the Marlins, who already were entertaining
proposals from a sizable group of suitors, but they made
it clear in negotiations that there would be no discounts
with Yelich. Not knowing what other clubs might be
offering, Stearns knew he'd have to put together an
impressive group of top prospects to get Miami to bite.

Yelich already had shown offensive potential while
also earning a Gold Glove in left field for Miami. Playing
in cavernous Marlins Park, with some of the deepest

outfield dimensions in the NL, he had not displayed eye-popping power, producing 18 home runs during the '17 season, including a modest seven in 76 games at home.

But Stearns knew the ball carried much better in Miller Park, particularly to the gap in right-center. He watched left-handed sluggers Travis Shaw and Eric Thames send drives over the fences with relative ease that year and figured Yelich's power numbers also would soar while wearing the home uniform of the Brewers. And, boy, was Stearns right.

To fend off other suitors and get the Marlins to do the deal, Stearns knew he had to put together the best possible package of prospects without completely gutting the top of his highly regarded farm system. Outfielder Lewis Brinson, recognized as the organization's top prospect, would have to be included, no matter how painful to part with him.

Two other top prospects, infielder Isan Diaz and outfielder Monte Harrison, were put in the deal, and to make the Marlins feel even better about the trade, a fourth player, right-hander Jordan Yamamoto, was added.

"We didn't take lightly the prospects we were trading," Stearns said. "But to get a player like Christian, you have to give up a lot. This deal didn't come at a cost of money, but it did with a cost of prospects."

As difficult as it was to trade Brinson and Harrison, Stearns and his staff knew they would be getting five years of control of both Yelich and Cain. Braun still had three years remaining on his contract, so Brinson and Harrison would have nowhere to play in the majors for Milwaukee, making it more palatable to part with them. The Brewers also had returning outfielders Domingo Santana and Keon Broxton, who combined for 50 home runs in 2017, and now likely would be on the bench, or back in the minors.

As usual when the team made a significant personnel move, media relations director Mike Vassallo arranged for Stearns to do a conference call with beat writers to answer questions after the Yelich trade was announced. Stearns is famously tight-lipped about moves before the club makes them official but while talking with reporters on that call, he provided a tip to expect another significant move the next day.

"Do you mean the signing of Lorenzo Cain?" Adam McCalvy of MLB.com said to Stearns.

As so often happens, news of the signing was revealed on Twitter by one of the many national baseball writers who do that so well. Stearns couldn't have been completely surprised but blurted out, "Oh, that's out there already?"

That signing wouldn't become official until Cain passed the requisite physical exam the next day but, in reality, Stearns added two tremendous difference makers within hours of each other. Before the second deal was done, however, Stearns had to convince Attanasio to sign off on both acquisitions.

"If we get one, do we really need the other?" Attanasio asked his general manager, realizing the significant investments in both money and prospects.

"Getting one just wants me to get the other even more," Stearns replied to his boss.

And, so, the course of the franchise was dramatically changed, certainly for the 2018 season. Management always takes its cues from the team's performance on the field as to what moves should come next, and after the rebuilding Brewers surprisingly came so close to making the playoffs the previous season, Attanasio and Stearns put their heads together and decided to go for it.

Acquiring Yelich and Cain certainly qualified as going for it. It shocked the baseball world and energized the team and its fans, who never saw it coming. January 25, 2018 will always be known as a watershed day in the history of the Brewers, a day that officially ended the rebuilding process and signaled a return to playoff mode.

In the understatement of the year, Stearns had this to say 10 months later about Cain and Yelich: "It's safe to say they both exceeded expectations."

CHAPTER TWO

Decisions, decisions, decisions

"What are you going to do with all of these outfielders?"

It was a question Brewers manager Craig Counsell heard many times in the days leading up to spring training. And it didn't stop when pitchers and catchers reported to camp ahead of the outfielders at Maryvale Baseball Park in Phoenix.

Counsell seemed puzzled and amused, and just a little bit irritated, that inquiring minds were making such a fuss about his outfield surplus. No manager in the history of the game had complained about having too many good players at his disposal, and Counsell wasn't about to become the first.

But, the question actually was a good one. With the additions of Christian Yelich and Lorenzo Cain, the Brewer's outfield cup runneth over. The starting trio figured to be Ryan Braun in left, Cain in center and Yelich in right. So where did that leave Domingo Santana, the starting right fielder in 2017, and Keon Broxton, a superb defender in center who played in 143 games that season? And that didn't even include Brett Phillips, one of the top prospects in the organization who stole time away from Broxton in center the previous September with a strong showing as the Brewers battled to stay in the playoff race.

Counsell came up with a rather surprising plan to try to ease the logjam. He announced Braun would see some action at first base during exhibition season to see how he looked there. Braun was a talented athlete who began his big-league career at third base but made so many errors during his 2007 Rookie of the Year season he was moved to the outfield and had remained there exclusively.

Incumbent first baseman Eric Thames, a left-handed slugger with prodigious power, became an overnight sensation the previous season by returning from three years in South Korea to bop 11 home runs in the month of April, a club record. Thames captured the imagination of the baseball world with that stunning power display but also seemed to catch the attention of those running the Major League Baseball drug program.

Thames often showed up at his locker for post-game interviews with a Band-Aid in the crook of his elbow, the tell-tale sign of another blood test for PEDs. After being tested three times within an 11-day period that April, the good-natured Thames smiled and delivered one of the quotes of the year to reporters.

"If people keep thinking I'm on stuff, I'll be here every day. I have a lot of blood and urine," Thames proclaimed.

Reporters couldn't tweet that one out fast enough for the rest of the world to see.

Built like a professional bodybuilder, Thames went on to hit 31 home runs for the season. He treated members of the Cincinnati Reds pitching staff as his personal punching bags, knocking 10 balls out of the park, most ever by a Brewers player against one club.

Behind Thames at first base was another powerful slugger, Jesús Aguilar, a perfect complement from the right side of the plate. A waiver claim from Cleveland shortly before camp opened in 2017, Aguilar forced his way onto the club that spring by ripping seven homers and driving in 19 runs in 25 games during exhibition season.

The affable giant – Aguilar tipped the scales at just under 300 pounds – proved a valuable player off the bench that season with 16 home runs and 52 RBI. If Braun was going to serve as a right-handed alternative to Thames at first base, Aguilar figured to lose playing time, making some wonder if there would be room for him on the big-league roster.

Upon arriving in camp, Braun, who had been informed beforehand by Counsell that he would get some action at first base, told reporters he already ordered the proper gloves to play the position. But he admitted to needing to hunt down another essential piece of equipment.

"I don't know if this is R-rated, but in the outfield, not too many guys wear a (protective) cup," Braun said, referring to the manner in which infielders protect the family jewels from hard-hit, bad-hop grounders. "I haven't worn a cup in over 10 years. I'll have to get one of those before I get super comfortable taking ground balls again."

To his credit, Braun willingly participated in the spring-training experiment. He always took pride in needing relatively little game action to prepare for the regular season, including far fewer at-bats than most players wanted, so his participation in exhibition action normally was sparse. But Braun would have to be tested at first base in real competition, so after a few days of workouts he made his debut at first base.

Despite dealing with health issues in recent years, particularly stiffness in his lower back, Braun had the physical talent to play first base. But he readily admitted to needing a crash course on the nuances of the position, such as proper positioning on cut-offs and rundowns, being alert for pickoffs and making flips to pitchers covering the bag on grounders to first.

In other words, there's more to playing first base than the average fan realizes. In the early stages of the experiment, Braun told beat writers covering the team, "I don't feel remotely comfortable now. I'm doing the best I can with it.

"Ultimately, if you want to get where we want to be as a team, based on the roster we've put together, it makes us a better team if I'm able to play multiple positions. I'm doing it with the understanding that it's in the best interests of the team. But, certainly, it feels awkward and uncomfortable at times."

And, so it went. One thing was clear, though Counsell was careful not to say it for public consumption. Yelich and Cain were going to play on an everyday basis. The Brewers did not spend $80 million on Cain and trade some of the organization's best prospects for Yelich to have them sit on the bench. And Braun, by virtue of his $18 million salary and past production, wasn't a part-timer, either. Nor, as it turned out, was he going to see a ton of action at first base.

One reason Counsell figured he could make the outfield situation work was his somewhat secretive plan to give Braun scheduled days off during the season. As often happens with players in their 30s, Braun was experiencing more health issues, particularly following lower-back surgery after the 2015 season. Braun also would need periodic cryotherapy procedures to address pain associated with a chronic nerve issue in his right thumb.

Braun had not played more than 140 games since the 2012 season, when he took the field 154 times. In 2016, his action dropped to 135 games, with an even further decline to 104 games in '17. That reduction in playing time, combined with occasional duty at first base, would create opportunities for other outfielders to crack the lineup.

Upon taking over as Brewers GM in October 2015, David Stearns stated what would become an oft-repeated mantra of focusing on "acquiring, developing and retaining young, controllable talent," and he would make move after move with that goal in mind. But preserving depth would be just as important, whether there was enough playing time for all involved or not. Santana, Broxton and Phillips all had minor-league options remaining, providing the roster flexibility that Stearns worked so hard to develop.

As camp progressed, even with Braun dabbling at first base, it became evident that some of those options would have to be exercised. But Aguilar was out of options, and after his important production off the bench in '17, the Brewers knew there was no way he would clear waivers if they tried to send him outright to the minors.

A factor the Brewers did not take lightly was the influence Aguilar quickly established in a tight-knit clubhouse with a growing number of Latino players. With a wry sense of humor, an affable nature and a presence that was large beyond his physical size, he quickly became a quiet leader in that group, and teammates were pulling for him to make the 25-man roster.

"He added some great things right off the bat and he played well, and I think for every player that kind of gives you a voice," Counsell said. "It was kind of the perfect storm in that way."

The Venezuelan native was not fluent in English but willingly used it in casual conversations with reporters in the clubhouse. In more formal interview sessions, he relied on the team's translator, Carlos Brizuela, to fully answer questions. Aguilar didn't make a big deal about it but you could see he was concerned about securing a roster spot with the team that had given him a chance to play in the majors after years of being buried in Cleveland's farm system.

"It's because you think, 'What's going to happen to me?'" Aguilar confided one day to Milwaukee Journal Sentinel reporter Todd Rosiak. "Especially when you come from a good year.

"But it's baseball. It is what it is. They try to win more games and battle for the title, and if I'm part of the team, it's going to be great. If not, I keep moving forward."

Making the roster puzzle even more difficult to piece together, yet another slugger was in the picture at first base in spring training. Ji-Man Choi, a native of South Korea, had been signed as a free agent over the winter, primarily to give the Brewers a productive first baseman at Class AAA Colorado Springs. But somebody forget to tell the always-smiling Choi that he wasn't supposed to make the big-league roster in camp.

Every time he was given a chance to play, Choi seemed to produce, showing the power that attracted the Brewers to him in the first place. In his first 25 Cactus League at-bats, Choi pounded three doubles and two home runs, knocking in eight runs with a gaudy 1.439 OPS. He quickly opened the eyes of Counsell and his coaching staff, who knew left-handed power did not grow on trees.

Though needing a translator supplied by the club to hold detailed discussions in English, the expressive Choi quickly became a favorite of teammates in the Maryvale clubhouse. With reliever Jeremy Jeffress serving the role of team disc jockey, loud music often filled the cozy dressing space and dance parties sometimes broke out, with Choi shaking his booty to the delight of others.

"I really enjoy the atmosphere," Choi told reporters. "I feel like it's a perfect fit for my personality. I wasn't sure what to expect at first. I love the way everyone goes about things professionally but also have the balance to goof around and play around. I really like it here."

So, beyond the logjam of outfielders the Brewers had to contemplate, the crowd was growing at first base with Thames, Aguilar, Choi and Braun. Depending on whether the Brewers opened the season with 12 or 13 pitchers, spots on the bench were hardly plentiful.

The final days of camp are always tense for players on the bubble, and Santana, Broxton, Phillips, Aguilar and Choi were on pins and needles, awaiting the final roster decisions. Broxton and Phillips got the inevitable news that they were being optioned to Colorado Springs. It had become evident two outfielders had to go but Broxton was so upset by being sent out he declined to speak with reporters.

As it turned out, Aguilar had nothing to worry about. The Brewers weren't about to cut a slugger with his kind of impact off the bench. But, in a surprise move, Choi also was added to the Opening Day roster by carrying one less reliever than originally expected. As it turned out, Choi's stay would be short. Very short.

The roster game can be cruel at times for players, and as the Brewers went through Houston for a couple of exhibition games en route to the opener in San Diego, word leaked they had picked up veteran lefty reliever Dan Jennings, who had been cut by Tampa Bay in a cost-cutting move. Jennings would not join the club until the second day in San Diego, giving a stay of execution for one player.

That player, as suspected, turned out to be Choi, and it didn't matter that he played a huge role in the Brewers' 2-1, 12-inning victory in the opener against the Padres. Choi came off the bench with two outs in the 12th to deliver a ringing double, setting the stage for Orlando Arcia's tie-breaking single.

As with many components of the game in the new age of analytics, roster management was becoming much more fluid. Stearns and Counsell talked about having the best 25 players to win the game that day, and keeping Choi for the opener proved to be genius.

"That turned out to be the best thing," Counsell said afterward. "It's kind of proof that you try to put the best roster together for every single game."

That fluid method of managing a roster can be cruel to players on the wrong end of the transactions, however. When Choi reported back to the ballpark the next day, he was informed he was being sent to Colorado Springs to make room to add Jennings to the bullpen. Yesterday's star had become today's optioned player. Nobody ever said the game was fair.

"He was disappointed, but I would be disappointed, too," Stearns said after delivering the tough news to Choi. "I would expect our players to be disappointed when they are being sent down to the minors.

"Look, he knows he's a major league-caliber player. We've made that clear to him on a variety of fronts, and he's going to be back here."

As it turned out, that move proved to be a sign of things to come for Choi. On June 9 in Philadelphia, he came off the bench to slug his first major-league grand slam, propelling the Brewers to a 12-3 victory over the Phillies. The next day, Choi was traded to Tampa Bay for infielder Brad Miller.

Hero today, gone tomorrow.

CHAPTER THREE

The dreaded Cubs

The only thing Brewers fans hate more than losing to the Chicago Cubs is losing to them at home, with vocal Chicago fans comprising at least half of the crowd, and often more. When the Cubs were going through a massive rebuilding project from 2011-'15 and losing gobs of games, their fans weren't as inclined to make the drive up I-94 to Milwaukee, where tickets were cheaper, parking easier and the retractable roof assuring creature comfort.

When the Cubs became good, very good, resulting in their first World Series triumph in 108 years to cap the 2016 season, that dynamic changed. Chicago fans quickly snapped up tickets, including prime seats, on the secondary market from Brewers fans who preferred to make some extra spending cash rather than sit next to a Cubs fan enjoying himself or herself.

At times, it was difficult to tell which team was wearing the home uniforms. The roar often was more deafening when a Cubs hitter delivered a big hit than when a Brewers hitter did so, and Milwaukee's ballpark soon became known as Wrigley Field North. The parking lots were filled with Illinois license plates, much to the consternation of loyal Brewers tailgaters who did not welcome the company.

Those Brewers fans who did not sell their tickets to interlopers from south of the Wisconsin/Illinois border sat mostly in misery on the opening home stand as Chicago recorded three victories in the four-game series. Injury was added to insult in the opener, an 8-0 thumping by the Cubs, when Brewers closer Corey Knebel went down as if he were shot on the mound, suffering a significant hamstring injury while throwing a pitch.

Why was the closer pitching in a lop-sided defeat, critics quickly asked? Knebel hadn't pitched in six days and needed some work to stay sharp, so manager Craig Counsell assigned him the top of the ninth inning despite the Brewers being down by eight runs. That little detail only made it more frustrating as Knebel was placed on the disabled list for possibly two months or more. It seemed a crippling blow at the time for the bullpen, but it would prove to be anything but that. Far from it.

The Brewers quickly recovered from that series setback and went on an eight-game winning streak, taking advantage of a soft stretch in their schedule against bottom feeders Cincinnati, Miami and Kansas City. But their early-season torment by the Cubs was not complete. That winning streak was snapped in frustrating fashion when the Brewers arrived at Wrigley Field on April 26 for a four-game series.

Those who have attended games at Wrigley in April – and May, for that matter – will tell you the conditions can be brutal. When the wind blows in off Lake Michigan that time of year, it can take your breath away, and no amount of layering of clothing makes it comfortable. All you need to do is look at the flags flying above the manual scoreboard atop the center-field bleachers to know what kind of day it will be.

Flags flying out, semi-tolerable. Flags flying in, welcome to the arctic circle, baseball style.

The series opener was a night game, making conditions worse as the sun set and temperatures dipped. With the wind howling in and knocking down every fly ball, it was evident from the outset that runs would be at a premium as Milwaukee's Chase Anderson and Chicago's Kyle Hendricks quickly settled into a pitcher's duel.

On this night, it would take a laser beam to get out of Wrigley, and Cubs slugger Kyle Schwarber delivered one in the bottom of the sixth. His scorching liner was just high enough to clear the wall in right field, cutting through the stiff breeze, for what would be the only run of the game.

Afterward, Cubs manager Joe Maddon would joke of Schwarber's homer, "His launch angle was perfect."

And, so, the tone was set for the entire series. It was no secret that the Brewers' offense was home-run dependent, despite the additions of Christian Yelich and Lorenzo Cain during the off-season. With the wind howling in all weekend, the Brewers' collective power was negated and they were shut out three times, managing only two runs, both coming in a 3-2 loss in the second game.

To be fair, Chicago's power was negated as well, with Schwarber delivering the only home run of the series. The Brewers hoped to be better in 2018 at manufacturing runs and not relying solely on the long ball to score. That would not be the case in this series, and in the process the Brewers wasted some excellent work by their underrated pitching staff.

The offensive frustrations peaked in the seventh inning of the Game 2 loss when Yelich faced left-handed reliever Brian Duensing with the bases loaded and absolutely crushed a drive to right. On any other day, it would have been a game-turning, and perhaps series turning, grand slam but with a gale blowing in from that direction, Yelich settled for a game-tying sacrifice fly. He made a dejected right turn at first base and returned to the visiting dugout, shaking his head in disbelief.

A 3-0 loss in the third game should not have come as a shock to either the Brewers or their fans. On the mound for Chicago was lefty Jose Quintana, who in less than a year with the club had become known as a Brewers killer. Making that development tougher to stomach, Milwaukee had tried to acquire Quintana from the Chicago White Sox before the 2017 trade deadline, only to see the Cubs jump in with a better offer, including top prospect Eloy Jimenez.

By blanking the Brewers on two hits over seven innings, Quintana extended his scoreless streak against them to 24 innings, including six in his earlier April start at Miller Park. In six outings against Milwaukee since being acquired by Chicago, Quintana was 4-1 with a 0.63 ERA. Making his dominance against the Brewers more confounding, he was 0-1 with a 11.19 ERA in his other three starts that month.

It wasn't as if Quintana was a flame-thrower with a high 90s fastball, or some other devilish pitch that gave hitters no chance. He used average velocity, great location and an effective changeup to get Brewers hitters to swing at pitches out of the strike zone, basically getting themselves out. And they seemed totally helpless to make adjustments.

Once again, Counsell was asked by reporters why Quintana looked like Sandy Koufax, Warren Spahn and Randy Johnson, all rolled into one against the Brewers, yet was just another pitcher when facing other opponents. The answer, Counsell insisted, was simple.

"He has commanded his fastball well against us, in and out," Counsell explained. "That's been the key to his success. It's the foundation for everybody. I'd give him some credit. He has pitched very well against us."

But it wasn't just Quintana mowing down the Brewers for the Cubs. The next day, Tyler Chatwood followed suit in a 2-0 victory, the third blanking in the series. Amazingly, the Brewers failed to score a single run against four Chicago starting pitchers, covering 27 innings. Yes, weather conditions were brutal, more conducive to football than baseball, but the Cubs managed to scratch out nine runs, good enough for four victories.

The Brewers roared into town on an eight-game winning streak, during which they averaged 5.63 runs per game. They limped out of town wondering where their offense had gone, even with the frigid north wind howling off the lake. Such is baseball. Momentum in baseball starts and ends 60 feet 6 inches from home plate, where the pitching mound is located.

Counsell played down the no-show by his hitters, keeping in mind the pitcher-friendly conditions in the series. Always one to keep an even keel and guide his team with patience, the savvy manager knew his players took their cue from him. If he pushed the panic button, they might start to doubt themselves. Instead, Counsell attributed the poor showing to the elements, and a victory the next day in Cincinnati left the Brewers with a respectable 17-13 record entering May.

Still, combined with the earlier series in Milwaukee, the Brewers were 1-7 against the Cubs, getting shut out five times. It was no secret that the NL Central title went through Chicago, and this was hardly the kind of showing the Brewers wanted against the two-time defending champs. If the Brewers were making any headway in closing ground against their rivals, it wasn't evident one month into the season.

That trend would flip before the season was done, in a notable way. And just in the nick of time.

CHAPTER FOUR

A timely injury

Good teams are able to overcome injuries, even to their best players. General manager David Stearns had worked hard since the team's large-scale rebuild began in 2015 to build as much depth as possible to ward off such issues. He often would trade one player for two, or two for three, continuing to build depth at both the big-league and minor-league levels.

The Brewers already had suffered one key injury in the early going when closer Corey Knebel blew out his hamstring against the Cubs. Quite often in baseball, injuries happen on seemingly routine plays. Knebel was merely delivering a pitch to the plate when he crumpled to the ground.

First baseman Eric Thames, the home-run sensation of the previous April, dove to his right to snag a grounder off the bat of Kansas City's Mike Moustakas in the eighth inning of the Brewers' game at Kauffman Stadium on April 24, the opener of a two-game interleague series. It was a play that first basemen routinely make without incident, and Thames flipped to reliever Dan Jennings covering the bag for the out.

Thames immediately knew it was anything but a routine play, however. Despite the extra length and protection of wearing a large first baseman's mitt, he felt his left thumb bend backward, creating an immediate burning sensation.

"I knew it was serious," said Thames, who sat stunned in the visiting clubhouse afterward, eating with one hand while holding his left hand upward, thumb immobilized. "I didn't feel a 'pop' but I knew something was up. You can't really control it."

An MRI the next morning confirmed everyone's worst fears, particularly those of Thames. He had a torn ulnar collateral ligament in the thumb, which would require surgery to repair. The prognosis was for a six to eight-week absence, meaning the Brewers would be without Thames for most of the remainder of the first half of the season. His left-handed power would be missed but, as it turns out, it was the best thing that could have happened for backup Jesús Aguilar.

This is why Stearns and his staff put so much emphasis on building depth, and why there was no way Aguilar was going to be placed on waivers at the end of spring training, roster squeeze or not. Manager Craig Counsell said he was glad that left fielder Ryan Braun was given training at first base but this was Aguilar's chance to prove the job should be his.

Before being claimed off waivers prior to spring training in 2017, Aguilar had been trapped in Cleveland's farm system, blocked in the majors by veterans such as Mike Napoli, Nick Swisher and Carlos Santana. The Indians were in contending mode in the AL Central and in no position to give an unproven player a good look at first base.

So, Aguilar found himself stuck at Class AAA Columbus, where he continued to post impressive power numbers with no reward. From 2014-'16, Aguilar slugged 68 home runs and drove in 262 runs. In '16, he led the International League with 30 home runs and 92 RBI. Over those three seasons, he was given a mere 58 at-bats at the major-league level, hardly enough of a sample size to tell whether he could succeed.

"I was doing everything I could do but they never gave me a chance," Aguilar said. "It was frustrating."

This is where pro scouting is so important for an organization. The Brewers' scouts had put in good reports on Aguilar, obviously focusing on his prolific power. The organization's eyes in Venezuela also saw the right-handed-hitting slugger post big numbers in his country's winter ball league, batting .314 with 10 home runs and 1.018 OPS in 42 games. The way the Brewers saw it, Aguilar was trending in the right direction at age 26.

When the Indians designated Aguilar for assignment to clear a roster space for corner infielder Richie Shaffer, the Brewers quickly filed a waiver claim, then waited to see if clubs in front of them in the process pecking order would pass. As it turns out, they did, and Aguilar was a Brewer.

Waiver claims can create an interesting paper trail, which was the case for Shaffer, a first-round draft pick of the Tampa Bay Rays out of Clemson in 2012. He was traded in November 2016 to Seattle in a five-player deal, then placed on waivers by the Mariners in December. Shaffer was claimed by the Philadelphia Phillies, who in turn placed him on waivers a week later. The Cincinnati Reds claimed him on December 23, only to waive him in early February.

So, in a matter of one offseason, Shaffer was a member of four organizations, none for whom he ever donned a uniform. He never played a game for Cleveland, either, before being released by the Indians in June 2018. Oddly enough, the Brewers signed Shaffer a month later and assigned him to Class AAA Colorado Springs but he never played in the majors for them before being granted free agency after the season.

To make room on their 40-man roster for Aguilar, the Brewers designated infielder Ehire Adrianza for assignment. They had claimed him only two days earlier from San Francisco and hoped he would clear waivers to be assigned to the minors. Alas, the Minnesota Twins, looking for infield help, claimed Adrianza, whose Brewers "career" lasted about 48 hours. Ehire, we hardly knew ye, literally.

As it turns out, the Indians should have kept Aguilar and passed on Shaffer but teams do not get do-overs on personnel moves. Hindsight is always 20-20 in such matters. To some, it appeared a somewhat curious move by the Brewers because they had signed Thames to a three-year deal out of South Korea only two months earlier, and Aguilar was a first baseman only.

Stearns and his staff never worried about such logistics, however. They looked for talent in agnostic fashion, remaining open to any and every move. Waiver claims came at the price of $100,000, a worthwhile gamble on a player whose primary calling card was prodigious power. Home-run hitters don't grow on trees, so Stearns figured why not?

Aguilar was quite productive off the Brewers' bench in 2017 (.265, 16 HRs, 52 RBI in 279 at-bats) but this was a completely different opportunity. With Thames on the shelf for a couple of months, he would get a chance to prove he could be an everyday contributor. Managers are no dummies, and when a player seizes the day and produces in a big way, he stays in the lineup.

And that's exactly what Aguilar did. He already had put together one of the greatest at-bats in recent club history, resulting in a 6-5 walk-off victory over Miami on April 21. Counsell called on Aguilar to pinch hit leading off the bottom of the ninth inning and he found immediate trouble, falling behind in the count, 0-2, against Marlins side-arming reliever Junichi Tazawa.

It was at that point that one of the most incredible pitcher-hitter battles you'll ever see began. After taking

First baseman Jesus Aguilar (24) receives a Gatorade bath from Hernan Perez (14) as he is mobbed by teammates after hitting a solo walk off home run that gave the Brewers a 6-5 win over the Miami Marlins on April 21st, 2018 at Miller Park.
AP PHOTO

a ball for a 1-2 count, Aguilar did whatever it took to stay alive as Tazawa threw the kitchen sink at him. He fouled off an inside fastball, then a curveball off the plate, barely getting a piece of it. After Aguilar fouled off a splitter, he took ball two, fouled off a 93-mph fastball and took another ball to make the count 3-2.

Aguilar fouled off another splitter, then a fastball, and yet another fastball. The battle had gone on for 12 pitches and more than six minutes, and Aguilar stepped out of the box to give both he and Tazawa a chance to catch their breath. The gassed reliever no longer was able to hit his spots, and pitch No. 13 was a fastball right down the middle that Aguilar did not miss.

Aguilar sent a long drive on a high arc toward right-center, a no-doubter off the bat. He looked over to the Brewers' dugout, where amazed and jubilant teammates began jumping over the railing and pouring on the field as the ball landed near a Toyota Highlander on a two-level display on the concourse. Had Aguilar's drive struck that vehicle, a fan would have received it free of charge. As Aguilar neared the waiting mob at home plate, he tossed his helmet into the air and jumped into the fray, getting pummeled and doused with anything not nailed down.

It was the most epic walk-off battle that anyone could remember seeing. It's one thing to stay alive for 13 pitches. It's another to end it with a monstrous, opposite-field, walk-off home run. It was the longest at-bat to result in a walk-off homer in the majors since September 1997, when the Angels' Garret Anderson did likewise on the 13th pitch against Minnesota.

Many sluggers are prolific swing-and-miss hitters, and Aguilar does have periods when he whiffs a lot. But one of the first things Counsell and his staff noticed about him in his first spring camp in '17 was solid plate discipline and the willingness to take pitches the other way. In other words, Aguilar was a hitter, not just a launcher of long balls, and his ability to stay alive at the plate kept the duel with Tazawa going.

"I've never seen anything like that," Counsell said in amazement afterward. "I've never seen anything better than that. It was a battle."

Asked if he could remember having an at-bat like that at any level, even in Little League back in Venezuela, an exhausted Aguilar smiled and said, "Not even in Nintendo."

For the remainder of the first half of the season, it sometimes appeared as if Aguilar were playing a video game. He put the offense on his broad shoulders over the next two months as the Brewers moved past the Cubs and into first place in the NL Central. Aguilar put together a strong May (eight HRs, 22 RBI, .920), then kicked it into another gear in June (10 HRs, 24 RBI, 1.099 OPS). He took over the league lead in homers and soared into the top pack in RBI.

The modest, fun-loving Aguilar quickly had become one of the most beloved players in the clubhouse, proving to be a perfect fit. He always put the team above himself, never beating his chest after a big game, always thanking his teammates for supporting him and doing likewise. He could mug with the best of them, putting on playful facial expressions in the dugout after home runs that TV cameras captured.

More important, Aguilar's confidence was growing. One of the oldest debates in baseball has been what comes first, success or confidence? But any hitter will tell you that you can't have the latter without the former. Aguilar always had believed in himself. He just wasn't sure he'd get the chance to prove he belonged. Given this opportunity, he didn't blow it.

Before you knew it, Aguilar was hearing All-Star chatter. What? A 2017 waiver claim making the 2018 All-Star team? Whoever heard of such a thing? But this was no dream. Aguilar had become one of the top run producers in the NL, and folks were taking notice. He wasn't voted onto the NL squad by fans or added as an extra in balloting by players, but Aguilar was placed on the "Final Vote" ballot, leaving it to fans to vote for one of five candidates.

The Brewers did not leave it to fans to figure out if Aguilar should make the All-Star team. The team's media relations and social media crew went to work behind the scenes to back Aguilar's candidacy in every creative way imaginable. Giant likenesses of Aguilar's head were made for promotional use, T-shirts with his image were distributed, coffee houses and doughnut shops gave away freebies. Aguilar footed the bill for a ticket giveaway to a game at Miller Park.

Teammates joined in the fun, promoting Aguilar every time a camera or microphone was pointed in their direction. They also took part in a massive social media campaign, and the team's blitz was wildly successful. Aguilar easily won the "Final Vote" with a total of 20.2 million votes, second-most ever since that campaign began. He finished ahead of four others from much larger markets – Los Angeles first baseman Max Muncy, San Francisco first baseman Brandon Belt, Washington shortstop Trea Turner and St. Louis third baseman Matt Carpenter.

"He's incredibly deserving," Counsell said of the unpretentious player simply known as "Aggie" in the clubhouse. "We're all thrilled for him."

Aguilar became the Brewers' fifth All-Star, joining outfielders Lorenzo Cain and Christian Yelich, and relievers Josh Hader and Jeremy Jeffress. Teammates, friends and family knew just how much it meant to the humble behemoth, who never allowed himself to think of being a major-league All-Star.

This wasn't a case of a player merely winning a popularity contest. With a .298 batting average, 24 home runs, 70 RBI and .995 OPS at the break, Aguilar earned his spot on the NL All-Star team. He eagerly accepted an invitation to the Home Run Derby, looking to soak in every drop of fun and excitement associated with the mid-season gala in Washington, D.C.

Aguilar wore a non-stop smile on his face in the days leading into the All-Star Game, taking every opportunity to thank those who voted for him.

"I'm really excited," he said. "I've just got to say thank you to all those (teammates) for the support. It was unbelievable for me, for my family. It's going to be my dream come true."

Aguilar would cool off considerably at the plate in the second half, showing some wear and tear of playing regularly for the first time in the majors. But the games in the first half of the season count the same as those in the pennant stretch, and for large periods of time, Aguilar carried the Brewers' offense. It was an unexpected performance that would not be forgotten by teammates or the front office.

And none of it would have happened if not for the thumb injury to Thames, who returned to active duty earlier than expected in mid-June, now a reserve player. Fair or not, Aguilar had stolen Thames' job during his absence, with no intention of relinquishing it.

CHAPTER FIVE

A merry month of May

Every contending team needs at least one strong month during the first half to put them in the middle of the fray, and for the Brewers that month was May. They went 17-13 in March/April, despite an ugly 1-7 showing in two series against the Cubs, keeping their collective heads above water despite serious injuries to closer Corey Knebel and first baseman Eric Thames.

It certainly didn't hurt that the Brewers began the month in Cincinnati, where the Reds seemed to be in perpetual rebuilding mode. They didn't have trouble scoring runs in hitter-friendly Great American Ball Park but Cincy's pitching staff usually struggled to prevent them. Injury-prone Homer Bailey lived up to his first name all too often, and the supposed staff ace would suffer an epically horrible 2018 season, going 1-14 with a 6.09 ERA, with 23 homers allowed in only 106 innings.

After beating Bailey, 7-6, in the second game of the series, the Brewers sent veteran left-hander Wade Miley to the mound on May 2, looking for a sweep in his delayed Milwaukee debut. Signed to a minor-league deal after spring training had opened, Miley had the club made with a strong showing in exhibition play, only to strain a groin fielding a bunt in his final outing. Instead of opening the season in the rotation, Miley was placed on the 15-day disabled list, for what would be a five-week stay.

Though it was a no-risk minor-league deal with a modest $2.5 million commitment, many people wondered why the Brewers were bothering with Miley. He was coming off one of the worst seasons of any major-league starter in 2017 with Baltimore, going 8-15 with a 5.61 ERA in 32 starts, including an alarming 1.729 WHIP (walks and hits per inning).

Miley's main issue was throwing strikes. In 157 1/3 innings, he walked 93 hitters, the highest total in the American League. But he also logged 142 strikeouts, indicating his stuff was still good when he got it over the plate. The Brewers also knew Miley had started throwing a cutter, a favorite of pitching coach Derek Johnson, who in only two seasons with the club had built a reputation of getting the most from his staff.

The understated Johnson preferred to stay behind the scenes, rarely doing interviews. In 11 seasons as pitching coach at Vanderbilt University, he helped build that program into a national power. He worked with several future major-league pitchers of note while there, including David Price, Sonny Gray, Jeremy Sowers, Jason Frasor and Mike Minor. A deep thinker who always seemed to find a way to help his pitchers, Johnson wrote "The Complete Guide to Pitching" in 2012, a manual that broke down every aspect of that art and was a must-read for any young hurler looking for success.

Johnson certainly was not a self-promoter but his pitchers spoke in glowing terms of what he did to make them better. He had left Vanderbilt to become minor-league pitching coordinator for the Chicago Cubs in 2013, earning a reputation in the game for his teaching ability. Upon building his coaching staff after becoming manager one month into the 2015 season, Craig Counsell often cited the importance of continuing to teach at the big-league level, and Johnson fit that mold perfectly.

To Miley's credit, he went back home to Louisiana after his miserable '17 season and reconnected with a former summer league pitching coach, Chris Westcott. The two made subtle adjustments in Miley's delivery that allowed him to throw more strikes, and the determined veteran incorporated those changes during encouraging mound sessions, looking more like the pitcher who won 16 games with Arizona in 2012.

Stearns had shown a willingness to look under every rock for talent during the Brewers' massive rebuilding process, and this was the prototypical buy-low situation. If Miley looked bad in exhibition competition, the Brewers could cut him with nothing ventured. But, if he threw the ball well, a predominantly right-handed staff would be augmented with a lefty with 200 major-league games under his belt.

The easy-going Miley had a refreshing honesty about his poor showing the previous season. Some players blame everybody but the mailman for their woes, but Miley knew he only had to look in the mirror to find the culprit.

"Last year was absurd," he told reporters after arriving at Maryvale Baseball Park. "You lose confidence in your stuff. I had lost my release point. I worked my tail off this off-season to try to get back mechanically to where I want to be. We'll see if it pays off."

One of the traits that made Stearns so successful in rebuilding his roster was an open mind, a willingness to consider anything and everything. Counsell shared that viewpoint, and he made it clear that Miley's struggles the previous season would play no role in how he was evaluated in camp.

"He had a tough year, so you want to try to help him, figure out different things he can do," Counsell said. "He's a guy who's had a lot of success in the league but has struggled a bit lately. He understands he has to make some changes for the next step of his career."

In that first outing against the Reds, Miley pitched six solid innings, allowing three hits and one run as the Brewers squeezed out a 3-1 victory for a three-game sweep. Baseball can be a cruel game at times, however, and Miley's return to action would be short-lived. In his next start against Cleveland at Miller Park, he grabbed his right side after throwing a pitch to Michael Brantley, the third hitter of the game.

Miley had suffered an oblique strain, a devilish injury for both pitchers and hitters because of the twisting and torqueing involved in throwing a pitch and swinging a bat. Miley would go back on the DL the next morning and would not throw another pitch for the Brewers for two months.

After sitting out five weeks with the groin strain, Miley failed to make it through two outings. But his season was far from over, and before all was said and done, he would make a huge impact with the Brewers.

Though unfortunate for Miley, his early exodus against the Indians led to one of the most remarkable moments of the season. He was replaced on the mound by left-hander Brent Suter, an overachieving soft-tosser who had carved a niche on the Brewers' roster as a swingman capable of starting and relieving, depending on the club's current needs.

Suter's fastball averaged a mere 85 mph, which should have made it nearly impossible to survive in the majors. But the Harvard graduate used smarts – he majored in both environmental science and public policy – including an uncanny ability to pitch up in the strike zone to keep hitters off-balance. On this night, however, Suter's biggest impact would come as a hitter.

Suter, who had five career hits, all singles, in 36 at-bats in the majors, came to the plate in the bottom of the third inning against Cleveland ace Corey Kluber, the reigning American League Cy Young Award winner. Taking a mighty yet controlled swing, Suter jumped on a first-pitch fastball and drove it out to center for a home run, an incredible blast estimated to have traveled 433 feet.

The drive stunned everyone, but none more than Kluber, who never had allowed a home run to an opposing pitcher. True, he hadn't faced a ton of them while pitching in the AL, facing them only in interleague competition, but still, this was unbelievable. It was one of those unexpected moments that defies explanation, and why baseball truly is the most unpredictable sport. There's an old saying in baseball that anyone with a bat in his hands can hit a home run. But that's mostly a saying.

No one on the Brewers' roster had more fun being a major-leaguer than the animated Suter, whose bubbly enthusiasm made him a favorite of teammates, not to mention media members who never knew what he might say or do next. Suter's nickname was "The Raptor" because of his penchant for stomping around in the clubhouse with hands thrust forward at shoulder level, imitating the walk of a Tyrannosaurus Rex.

Having no practice at home-run trots, Suter raced around the bases as if being chased out of Jurassic Park by ravenous dinosaurs. As might be expected, he returned to a raucous reception in the home dugout. No team had more fun celebrating homers than the Brewers, who put together a receiving line of teammates with arms raised for forearm bashes. By the time the home-run hitter got to the end of the dugout, he often was both exhilarated and exhausted.

Utility infielder Hernán Pérez added another feature at times, bringing confetti poppers into the dugout to shower the protagonist with streamers. Mardi Gras had nothing on the Brewers when it came to celebrating home runs.

"It was a lot of fun," the excitable Suter said. "There was confetti flying. Everybody was trying to take my helmet off. A lot of raptor noises. It was great. One of those things you'll never forget."

There was more good news that day when Knebel returned from his hamstring injury sooner than expected after a brief minor-league rehab stint. But there also would be a sobering development on the health front when an examination of catcher Stephen Vogt revealed he had suffered a career-threatening shoulder injury while also on minor-league rehab.

Vogt was acquired from Oakland at midseason in 2017 and quickly proved to be a valuable asset, on and off the field. He was an expert handler of pitchers, had some left-handed pop at the plate and exerted a tremendous veteran influence in an already-tight clubhouse. Vogt failed to make it out of spring training, however, suffering a shoulder strain that landed him on the DL.

The Brewers opted to keep Vogt at the end of camp despite that injury, guaranteeing his $3 million salary. That's how much they valued his offensive potential, leadership skills and steady presence. He had worked hard over the winter to strengthen his shoulder and improve his biggest flaw – throwing to bases – which made the injury even tougher to absorb.

Nearing the end of his rehab assignment with Class AA Biloxi, Vogt re-injured his shoulder making an off-balance snap throw to third base, trying to foil a stolen-base attempt. But this time he completely blew it out, suffering damage to the rotator cuff, labrum and shoulder capsule. An MRI confirmed the devastating injury, bringing Vogt to tears when talking to beat writers about it.

"The biggest emotion is sadness," said Vogt, usually an upbeat, positive person. "It's hard. I'm upset. I worked really hard my whole life and career to help win games. When you can't help your teammates win games on the field, it's really hard... It's definitely weighing on me."

Vogt would later undergo surgery and never played a game for the Brewers in 2018. To his credit, he remained with the team the rest of the season, providing support in the clubhouse and later in the dugout. True to form, he put his personal setback aside, realizing he might never play again, to be there for his teammates. A class act in every way.

In that same game against Cleveland, utility infielder Nick Franklin, just summoned from the minors to replace slump-ridden Eric Sogard, suffered a strained quadriceps running to first base in the fourth inning. Franklin would join Miley on the DL and never play in another game for the Brewers, taking so long to recover from what appeared to be a minor injury that management gave up on him.

And there was yet more bad news on the injury front. Middle infielder Mauricio Dubon, one of the top prospects in the organization, suffered a torn ACL in his left knee at Class AAA Colorado Springs while trying to escape a rundown on the bases. Dubon was riding a 23-game hitting streak at the time and certainly would have made his major-league debut at some point in the 2018 season, considering some of the misadventures to come in the Brewers' middle infield. Instead, he was done for the year.

Undaunted by such setbacks, the Brewers plowed forward through an increasingly tough May schedule, including an 11-day, 10-game odyssey through

Colorado, Arizona and Minnesota. The Brewers never had enjoyed much success in Coors Field but they kicked off that trip by taking three of four games from the Rockies, a series that was capped in stunning, historic fashion on Mother's Day.

The scheduled starter that Sunday, Chase Anderson, had become ill Saturday night with what he believed to be food poisoning. It was evident he would not be able to pitch the next day but conveniently, the Brewers' Class AAA affiliate was just down the road in Colorado Springs. The Brewers called manager Rick Sweet and told him to withhold Freddy Peralta from his scheduled Saturday start.

Instead of pitching for the Sky Sox, the 21-year-old Peralta would make his first major-league start against the Rockies. And it was a debut for the ages. With great deception and movement of an otherwise average fastball, he mesmerized Colorado's hitters, taking a no-hitter into the sixth inning and striking out 13 hitters before departing with two outs.

How incredible was that spur-of-the-moment performance? No Brewers pitcher had recorded that many strikeouts in a debut since July 28, 1997, when Steve Woodward whiffed 12 Toronto hitters over eight innings of a 1-0 victory.

What made Peralta's day even more memorable was his family story. His parents, who never had seen him pitch professionally in person, had traveled from the Dominican Republic to watch his scheduled start the previous evening in Colorado Springs. Instead, they accompanied their son to Denver to watch his remarkable debut against the Rockies.

As Counsell strolled to the mound to remove Peralta in the sixth inning, the infielders gathered on the mound to congratulate the skinny righty on his performance. As the pitcher walked off, the group on the mound spotted Peralta's parents and girlfriend in the stands beyond the visiting dugout, cheering with great emotion.

As Tom Hanks famously said as manager Jimmy Dugan in the movie "A League of Their Own," there's no crying in baseball. But first baseman Jesús Aguilar

Called on for an emergency start on Mother's Day, Freddy Peralta responded by taking a no-hitter into the sixth inning and finished with 13 strikeouts.
AP PHOTO

admitted afterward to tearing up as he watched Peralta's cheering section in action.

"I almost cried," Aguilar said. "They were so happy, so proud of their son. I was talking with (catcher Manny) Piña. I said, 'Let's cry. Why not?' It was close, I'm telling you."

In one of his first trades as general manager at the winter meetings in December 2015, Stearns sent power-hitting first baseman Adam Lind to Seattle for three teenage pitching prospects nobody had heard of. One of those youngsters was Freddy Peralta, who roared through the farm system faster than anyone could have anticipated, using that deceptive fastball to pile up strikeouts.

Of the 98 pitches he threw on Mother's Day, 89 were fastballs, an incredible ratio that a pitcher usually can't get away with at the big-league level. But Peralta really wasn't throwing the same fastball, pitch after pitch. In addition to his four-seamer that rides up in the strike zone, Peralta changed his grip at times to get cutter action, keeping Piña on his toes behind the plate.

With an unobstructed view from center field that day, Christian Yelich was amazed at the movement on Peralta's fastball, and quite happy he was not standing in the batter's box.

"It looked like it was moving five feet," Yelich said.

Peralta would struggle with control issues at times but no major-league club figured out how to hit his fastball as he went on to make 14 starts for the Brewers. Over 78 1/3 innings, he allowed a mere 49 hits while compiling 96 strikeouts, an encouraging first season for a young pitcher who proved valuable in filling voids created by injuries.

"He's always going to be looking for ways to get better and different ways to get hitters out," Counsell said. "I think what was clear is that he has a very special pitch. He gets swings and misses on balls thrown in the middle of the strike zone, which doesn't happen much in Major League Baseball."

The Brewers would go on to take two of three in Arizona and Minnesota on that trip, returning home with a 7-3 record. With a 5-2 home stand against the New York Mets and St. Louis Cardinals, they finished May with a 19-8 record, a strong showing, all things considered. The Brewers entered June in first place in the NL Central, four games ahead of the Cubs. Not too shabby.

CHAPTER SIX

The pen is mightier

Today's game of baseball is not the same game your father watched. Analytical evaluations of every facet of the game are being dissected 10 ways to Tuesday, resulting in many changes in game strategy. Hitters are taught to focus more on launch angles and exit velocities. Strikeouts are considered collateral damage to that power-ball approach.

With spray charts and hitter tendencies becoming part of the daily game preparation, defensive shifts became commonplace to stop batters from hitting them where they weren't. Left-handed pull hitters try to figure out where they're supposed to hit the ball with one infielder in shallow right field, another in the hole at second and yet another playing up the middle. What once were sure-fire hits have become hard-hit outs.

Analytics also cautioned against allowing your starting pitcher to go the third time through an opponent's lineup, unless your name is Clayton Kershaw, Corey Kluber, Max Scherzer or Madison Bumgarner, or someone of their ilk. No manager paid closer attention to that trend than the Brewers' Craig Counsell, who didn't hesitate to pull the plug after five or six innings, whether the starting pitcher was in trouble or not.

In fact, Counsell didn't use the terms "starters" and "relievers." The first pitcher to take the mound was the "initial out-getter." Those who followed were merely "out-getters." Counsell regularly cautioned members of the media against thinking in terms of "starters" and "relievers." Instead, he said the proper focus was getting 27 outs, no matter what it took to record them.

"What we talk about is, 'How are we going to get 27 outs tonight?'" Counsell explained. "That's what you have to do to win – get 27 outs."

Of course, "bullpenning" isn't worth a darn if you don't have a reliable relief corps. And, even with closer Corey Knebel's early-season hamstring injury, it became apparent quickly that one of the Brewers' strengths – if not THE strength – was their bullpen. In particular, Counsell had a one-of-a-kind weapon in a fire-balling left-hander by the name of Josh Hader.

One of four prospects acquired from Houston by previous general manager Doug Melvin in a trade for centerfielder Carlos Gomez and right-hander Mike Fiers, the lanky Hader was developed in the minors as a starting pitcher. When the Brewers were looking for left-handed help in their bullpen in June of 2017, however, Hader was summoned to the majors for the first time and eased into action in relief.

To say Hader took to that new role was like saying a polar bear prefers cooler weather. Slinging a mid-90s fastball with good movement from a three-quarters arm slot and burying left-handed hitters with a slider they had no chance of reaching, Hader was dominant from the outset. He made 35 appearances that season, posting a 2.08 ERA while allowing only 25 hits in 47 2/3 innings. Hader struck out 68 hitters, second-most among rookie relievers, and held opponents to a puny .156 batting average.

After that season, general manager David Stearns and Counsell said they would assess the team's needs and where Hader best fit to decide whether he would remain in the bullpen or return to starting. But there was never any indication they seriously considered fixing what wasn't broken. When the team reconvened in Phoenix for spring training, Hader remained in a relief role.

Stearns and Counsell knew Hader was more suited to bullpen duty in the majors than starting because he basically was a two-pitch pitcher – fastball and slider. He threw a changeup only on rare occasion, and rarely with games in the balance. Starters, or "initial out-getters," needed three pitches at a minimum, with the elite ones featuring four.

A stellar April earned Josh Hader NL Reliever of the Month honors. Hader would go on to strike out 143 hitters during the 2018 season, a major-league record for a left-handed reliever.
AP PHOTO

Because of Hader's starting background, Counsell realized that he could use him in a different fashion from most relievers. Hader was capable of pitching more than one inning, quite often covering two, making him a unique weapon in protecting leads. In tight games, Counsell saw no reason to hold Hader back for the final inning or two, often summoning him for the sixth or seventh, if not both.

In essence, Hader was the Brewers' mid-game closer, and he was darn good at it. Improving on his rookie showing from the previous season, Hader was virtually unhittable on most nights, piling up strikeouts as if he were playing fantasy baseball. It got so ridiculous that Hader quickly caught the attention of the national media outlets, especially after an unbelievable outing in Cincinnati on April 30.

Summoned with one out in the seventh inning and the Brewers clinging to a one-run lead, Hader provided a preview of things to come when he struck out Joey Votto on three pitches, something you rarely see happen. Votto is known for his plate discipline and pitch recognition, with incredible hand-eye coordination that keeps strikeouts to a minimum, but he had absolutely no chance against Hader, going down on a fastball and two filthy sliders.

And thus it began. Hader struck out Scott Schebler on four pitches to finish the seventh, then opened the bottom of the eighth by whiffing Eugenio Suarez on four pitches. After a temporary loss of command led to a five-pitch walk of Tucker Barnhart, Hader mowed down Alex Blandino on four pitches and pinch-hitter Adam Duvall on three. Of Hader's 16 pitches that inning, all but one were fastballs. No trickery. Here it is. Try to hit it.

Hader said he was good to stay in the game in the ninth and Counsell wasn't about to argue. Realizing he had little chance to hit Hader, speedster Billy Hamilton tried bunting with two strikes and fouled off the pitch, becoming strikeout No. 6. Jesse Winker made Hader throw six pitches before waving futilely at an 83-mph slider.

With Votto standing in the on-deck circle, Hader did him a favor by blowing a 95-mph fastball by Jose Peraza to end the 6-5 victory. Hader had recorded eight outs on 37 pitches, all via strikeouts. No one had seen anything like it because in the history of the game, no reliever had done such a thing.

Struggling for words to describe Hader's outing, Counsell said, "Literally, your mouth is kind of wide-open, watching it. It was absolutely incredible."

The soft-spoken Hader is about as aw-shucks as they come, and the last player on the planet to brag about himself. Any other relief pitcher who ended a game with eight strikeouts would have bragged a little bit but not Hader, who made it seem like another night at the office.

Asked to sum up the outing, Hader simply said, "Fun. A lot of fun. Just really staying on my strengths and sticking with what's working."

At that point, Hader had made 11 appearances, logging a remarkable 39 strikeouts in 18 innings. He had four saves of at least two innings, a 1.00 ERA and 0.50 WHIP. Hader would go on to post more mind-boggling numbers over the first half of the season, including 89 strikeouts in 48 innings, a stunning ratio of 16.7 per nine innings. Those numbers made him an easy choice for his first All-Star selection.

Before the season was done, Hader would strike out 143 hitters, a major-league record for a left-handed reliever and franchise mark for any reliever, righty or lefty. He made 23 appearances of at least two innings, and the Brewers won every one of those games.

Because Counsell often used Hader for multiple innings, he knew he'd have to protect one of the best arms in the organization with two or three days off afterward. At times, that unavailability infuriated misguided fans who thought other victories slipped away that Hader could have saved. But Counsell knew what he was doing and stuck to his guns. Hader made 55 appearances during the season and the Brewers' record in those games was 48-7. Difficult to argue with that kind of success, but some folks did anyway.

Normally easy-going and willing to explain the reasons for the way he managed games, Counsell became frustrated with the constant questions about his use of Hader. Before a game in early September in Washington, he said he'd explain for the last time why Hader had to have days off after pitching.

"Every arm is different; every player is different," Counsell said. "Everybody recovers different. I think the questions about Josh are because he's used in a non-traditional way. I think that's what's got everybody freaked out. We've tried to find a way to take Josh's talents and make him as good as he can be, as effective as he can be."

What Counsell didn't say for public consumption was that Hader was requesting more time off between outings as the season wore on. He packed only 180 pounds on his lanky 6-3 frame and needed more recovery time while logging more innings than any other reliever in the National League.

Every day before games, the relievers go out and play catch to test how their arms feel. Counsell and his pitching coaches, Derek Johnson and Lee Tunnell, then would check in with each one to gauge their availability for that game. Few relievers ever said "no" but Counsell and his coaches could tell from body language and/or the wording of responses if a pitcher needed a day off, and even in a pennant race, the Brewers weren't going to abuse Hader.

"This is what we think is the best way for Josh," Counsell explained further. "This is getting maddening. I'm really done explaining it. He can't pitch every day. He can't drive the bus. He can't serve the food in the room. He can't do it all. I know we want him to do it all but he's not going to do it all."

No reporter dared ask Counsell about Hader's use the rest of the season.

On the other end of the experience spectrum from Hader was Jeremy Jeffress, a veteran right-hander who in his own way was having an equally brilliant season. He was 30 when the season began and had played in all or parts of eight seasons in the majors, and was in his third go-round with the Brewers.

Jeffress' career got off to a fitful start due to substance abuse problems, in particular, marijuana use. It would take years for doctors to figure out he suffered from epilepsy and was self-medicating, making it more difficult to succeed as a major-league pitcher.

The Brewers included Jeffress, then one of their better pitching prospects, in the December 2010 trade with Kansas City for ace Zack Greinke. From there, he was traded to Toronto and released, re-signing with Milwaukee during the 2014 seasons.

Jeffress, whose repertoire in the early years consisted mostly of a live fastball and electric, over-the-top curveball, kicked his career into a higher gear with the Brewers in 2015, posting a 2.65 ERA over a workhorse 72 outings. He took it a step farther, excelling as the team's closer before Stearns packaged him with catcher

Jonathan Lucroy in a trade with Texas, netting three top prospects as part of the rebuilding of the organization.

Jeffress would have more off-field issues with the Rangers, including a DUI arrest, before being reacquired in a trade-deadline deal on July 31, 2017. He made no secret of his glee in returning to the Brewers, because he never succeeded with other clubs as he did with Milwaukee. The numbers were impossible to ignore: entering the '18 season, Jeffress was 4-3 with a 4.76 ERA and one save in 91 games with Kansas City, Toronto and Texas; and 13-3 with a 2.56 ERA and 27 saves in 180 games with the Brewers.

Realizing his comfort level with Milwaukee was the key to success, Jeffress took a pay cut from his $2.2 million salary in '17 to sign a $1.7 million contract with two club options that included no buyouts. The money was not guaranteed, and Jeffress' agent, Joshua Kusnick, received significant pushback from the players' union for accepting such a deal. But Kusnick knew the best chance for Jeffress to succeed was with the Brewers, and the pitcher was confident he'd make the club and guarantee his salary.

Jeffress was not the same pitcher the Brewers dealt to Kansas City seven years earlier. He learned a split-finger changeup grip from teammate Junior Guerra, a weapon he used with tremendous effectiveness as an "out" pitch. Hitters feared getting behind in the count and having to deal with that pitch, which darted downward in the strike zone, making them look silly.

"It's just a different way to attack hitters," Jeffress explained. "You want to have as many weapons as possible. I'd just say I'm more mature and confident in the stuff I throw."

Jeffress got off to a sensational start to the season and never eased up, and Counsell began using him early and often. Jeffress' specialty was coming into games in what appeared to be hopeless situations, only to escape unscathed. He became the staff's Houdini, with no jam too daunting.

One such appearance came on April 22 against Miami at Miller Park, when Jeffress was summoned in relief of Guerra with the bases loaded and no outs. Jeffress dominated the next three hitters with a strikeout, foul pop and another strikeout, letting out a primeval roar as he stomped off the mound to a standing ovation.

And so it went for Jeffress, the bullpen's Swiss Army knife who put up impossible-to-ignore numbers en route to his first All-Star berth at age 30. In 46 first-half appearances, he posted a 6-1 record and 1.34 ERA while holding opponents to a .179 batting average with 50 strikeouts in 47 innings.

Counsell continued to call on Jeffress to bail out other pitchers, and he continued to do so. When all was said and done, he allowed a mere 8 of 38 inherited runners to score, retired the first batter he faced 50 of 73 times and compiled a 1.29 ERA, tops among qualifying relievers in NL.

Knebel would struggle with his command after returning from the DL before returning to dominant form when the team needed it most in September. The trio of Hader, Jeffress and Knebel would lead the way, in large part because of their uncanny ability to strike out hitters when needed most, but other relievers would make key contributions at different junctures, including Matt Albers, Taylor Williams and lefty specialist Dan Jennings.

An already stout bullpen got an unexpected boost just before the All-Star break with the arrival of right-hander Corbin Burnes, the top pitching prospect in the organization. A fourth-round draft pick in 2016 out of tiny St. Mary's (Calif.) College, Burnes quickly moved through the farm system with an impressive four-pitch repertoire and calm, confident demeanor while attacking hitters with an aggressive approach.

In what proved to be a stroke of genius, the Brewers had Burnes move from starting to a relief role in June at Class AAA Colorado Springs, figuring he might prove of use in Milwaukee's bullpen at some point. That moment came sooner than expected when Burnes was summoned and thrust into a July 10 game in Miami with the Brewers holding a 6-4 lead in the eighth inning. Showing no nervousness whatsoever, Burnes pitched two hitless innings to record a save in his very first game in the big leagues.

Counsell would reference that outing for the rest of the season as indication of how special Burnes was, and indeed, it proved to be a sign of things to come. Relievers rarely have the mix of pitches that Burnes featured and Counsell continued to use him in game-deciding situations with impressive results. In 30 appearances, Burnes posted a 7-0 record and 2.61 ERA, retiring the first batter he faced a remarkable 25 of 30 times.

The soft-spoken Johnson had the best analysis of what made Burnes special, saying, "It just boils down to he has a good heartbeat. He's not overwhelmed by the situation, even in the high-leverage spots."

Yet another dominant weapon had been added to an already formidable relief corps, and it was no surprise that Counsell nearly wore a path from dugout to mound, using his bullpen early and often. The pitching staff would record no complete games, and only a handful of times would an "initial out-getter" go eight innings.

The Brewers became Exhibit A for the benefits of "bullpening." You don't make it to the postseason by blowing late leads, which can cut the heart out of a team. Thanks to their deep and talented relief corps, you had a better chance of winning the lottery than beating the Brewers in late stages of games. Over the course of the season, they would take leads into the eighth inning 83 times. Eighty times, they emerged victorious.

To steal a quote from the late, great Yogi Berra, opponents would discover when facing the Brewers, it got late early.

CHAPTER SEVEN

Next man up

Over the course of the 162-game grind, every team suffers its share of injuries. The good teams are able to weather those storms and keep their heads above water until the cavalry arrives. Average teams are unable to do so, and eventually lose their way. And the bad teams have no chance whatsoever when the training room becomes standing room only.

Thanks in large part to general manager David Stearns' determined focus on building depth on his 40-man roster, and beyond, the Brewers were able to overcome an ongoing series of significant injuries to players expected to play key roles during the season. When players were sent to the minors at the end of spring training, Stearns and Counsell sat down with them in private and told them to stay ready, that they would be needed at some point. And the bosses meant it.

Three players expected to be on the Opening Day roster never made it out of spring training in one piece. Veteran catcher Stephen Vogt strained his throwing shoulder and didn't play an inning during exhibition season, opening a job for Jett Bandy. Boone Logan, a veteran left-handed specialist, or "loogie," in the bullpen, suffered a muscle strain behind his pitching shoulder and also opened on the disabled list.

One player expected to begin the season on the DL was right-hander Jimmy Nelson, who suffered a significant shoulder injury the previous September during a game against the Cubs at Wrigley Field. Making the blow-out even tougher to take, Nelson suffered the injury diving back to first base after a base hit, not throwing a pitch off the mound.

Nelson, a big, hard-throwing bulldog of a pitcher, had some fits and starts in the early years of his career but had come into his own over the second half of the 2017 season. After leading the league with 16 losses the previous year, he improved the command of his pitches after working with pitching coach Derek Johnson on a modified, shortened delivery, in essence, pitching from the stretch.

Making that adjustment led to dramatic results. Nelson led the staff with 17 quality starts, going 10-0 with a 1.69 ERA in those games. He struck out 199 hitters – by far the most of his career – in 175 1/3 innings, and the Brewers went 17-12 in his 29 starts. Nelson had become de facto ace of the staff, and there was good reason to believe the team would not have fallen one game short of the NL's second Wild Card playoff berth had Nelson not missed the final three weeks.

The hope was that Nelson would make it through his grueling, tedious rehabilitation process in time to pitch sometime during the season, most likely in the second half. But, given the extent of his shoulder injury, there was no way to know for sure when he'd be ready to pitch in a game again or what impact he might have.

Nelson was known for a ferocious work habit, which often reached frenetic paces, so the team's management knew he would attack his rehab program with a vengeance. In fact, the team's bosses and medical staff knew the biggest task would be pulling in the reins on Nelson and not letting him suffer setbacks by pushing too hard.

In mid-May, Nelson experienced what was described as a "rehab plateau," meaning he had stopped making progress in his throwing and exercise program. It was not uncommon for an athlete recovering from a serious injury to reach a stage of treading water, and Stearns was careful not to call the situation a setback.

Nelson had been so far ahead of schedule in the early months following surgery that there were hopes of nothing but smooth sailing but that is more the exception than the rule in such cases. Nelson had plateaued in his long-toss program off flat ground at a distance of 150 feet, and the decision was made to get a medical opinion from his surgeon, Los Angeles specialist Neal ElAttrache.

"This is just part of the process of rehab," Stearns cautioned reporters. "Occasionally, you have to go and get checkups. I don't think there's really a level of concern here. I'm sure Jimmy would like this to be moving faster but this is where we are right now."

Counsell also chose his words carefully, saying, "When we get ahead of schedule and then we kind of get back on schedule, we're at a plateau. It's important for everyone involved in the rehab process that we know we're still going in the right direction."

The Brewers refrained from the outset from putting a timeline on Nelson's return but there was hope that he would return at some point of the season and be tantamount to trading for a starting pitcher. Unfortunately, Johnson mentioned at the team's winter fan festival in late January that Nelson might be ready to pitch again in June, and when that didn't happen, some impatient fans accused management of being pollyannish.

As the weeks and months passed, it became evident that Nelson would not return to the mound during the season, despite his hard work and proper medical guidance. A general expectation for recovery from such an injury is 9 to 12 months, and it became apparent Nelson would fall on the back end.

In mid-August, with six weeks remaining in the season, the Brewers decided it finally was time to announce the inevitable, and take some pressure off Nelson in the process. Taking a closer look at where the pitcher was in his rehab program and how many games were left, Stearns conceded that Nelson would not pitch in 2018.

"I think it's fair to say that we're running short on time," Stearns told reporters before a game against the Cubs at Wrigley Field, where Nelson suffered his devastating injury. "We haven't closed the doors to anything at this point, but it's getting to the point where it's probably a little tougher to see Jimmy making a significant impact during the month of September."

Counsell was more blunt in his assessment of the situation, saying, "Jimmy pitching for us this year is unlikely. That's not due to a setback of any nature. That's just due to the pace of his rehab right now."

Added Stearns: "The point here is get a healthy Jimmy Nelson, for us and for his career, and we're willing for that to take as long as it needs to take."

As the 2017 season progressed, Nelson, Chase Anderson and Zach Davies emerged as the Brewers' top three starting pitchers, or "initial out-getters," if you will. Though not as effective as that season, Anderson still was taking regular turns in the rotation. Davies, however, never really got out of the starting blocks due to different health issues.

A finesse pitcher who relies on pinpoint command and mixing his pitches rather than velocity, Davies had gotten off to a slow start in '17 before finding a groove and finishing with a 17-9 record and 3.90 ERA. So, there was no real cause for alarm when he struggled through his first six starts (2-3, 4.24) of this season.

But Davies revealed to the medical staff that his shoulder was barking, leading to a diagnosis of rotator cuff inflammation. The slightly built righty was expected to miss only one start, two at the most, but his shoulder did not cooperate. Davies cut short a bullpen session designed to prepare him for his next start and went back into rehab protocol.

Davies would sit out a month before pitching in a game again, and his return would be short-lived. After two ineffective outings (14 hits, nine runs in nine innings), he was placed back on the DL. Davies would develop lower back issues in addition to his balky shoulder, keeping him on the sidelines for another three months and putting his frustration meter firmly in the red zone.

At approximately the same time that Davies was sidelined, left-hander Wade Miley returned from his groin injury, only to return to the DL with an oblique injury, leaving the Brewers shy two members of their starting rotation at the same time. Rookie Freddy Peralta, who made headlines with his sensational Mother's Day debut in Colorado, helped fill some of that injury void but there would be more bad news in late July.

Left-hander Brent Suter, a valuable swingman who always could be counted on to do what was needed, felt a pop in his pitching elbow during his July 22 start against the Los Angeles Dodgers at Miller Park, exiting after three innings as the Brewers were drubbed, 11-2. Suter had experienced forearm tightness a few weeks earlier but this time he knew it was something worse. Much worse, as it turned out.

The usually ebullient Suter, one of the most popular players in the clubhouse because of his fun-loving nature, comic impersonations and willingness to do whatever was best for the team, stunned reporters in the clubhouse after the game by actually apologizing for getting injured.

"I personally feel horrible right now for letting the team down by pitching badly and getting hurt again, said Suter, tears in his eyes. "In the clubhouse, we realize it's a long season. There's going to be ups and downs, and this is definitely a valley right now.

"Personally, I feel horrible. Just horrible."

An MRI the next morning confirmed the worst fears of Suter and the Brewers. He had a torn ulnar collateral ligament in his elbow, one of the biggest fears for pitchers yet an injury that had become much too commonplace in the game. Suter's season was over after 20 outings, including 18 starts. He was 8-7 with a 4.44 ERA, numbers that didn't reflect his true value to the pitching staff.

Beyond that, Suter knew he wouldn't pitch much in 2019, either, with the recovery time from Tommy John reconstructive surgery normally sidelining a pitcher for a year. When team doctor William Raasch broke the news to Suter, he broke down and cried. Later, he merely called it "a tough day."

"It's tough news," a somber Counsell said after news of Suter's plight was announced. "It's tough news for Brent, first of all. We're going to miss him. Unfortunately, it's a tough injury for a pitcher. Now, he's going to have to go through it and get through it."

At the outset of the season, most of the outside world thought the Brewers did not have enough starting pitching to contend for the NL Central title. At that time, there was no way to know that Nelson would never throw a pitch, that Davies would make only 13 starts, most of them ineffective (2-7, 4.77 ERA), that Miley would suffer two injuries that robbed him of half the season or that Suter would be lost before the end of July with a blown-out elbow.

Baseball people are quick to tell you that nobody feels sorry for you during the tough times, so the Brewers did not check their mailbox for sympathy cards. They merely asked the next man up to do his best. That's what Peralta did. Ditto for journeyman righty Junior Guerra, who finally ran out of gas in August. When all was said and done, 11 different pitchers would make starts.

Right-hander Jhoulys Chacín, an unheralded off-season pickup, was the only starter who did not miss a turn. Chacín was a revelation, rising to the occasion by posting a 15-8 record and 3.50 ERA in a career-high 35 starts. Every rotation needs an anchor, and the savvy veteran filled that role admirably in his first season with the Brewers.

Injuries, indeed, are part of the game. The good teams survive them. The Brewers were a good team.

CHAPTER EIGHT

Lost weekend in Pittsburgh

After roaring through May with a 19-8 record, the Brewers kept their collective feet on the accelerator as the All-Star break neared. They swept a three-game interleague series at home against the Minnesota Twins, then took three of four from the much-improved Atlanta Braves, a surprise contender in the NL East with an infusion of exciting, young talent.

The Cubs kept the pressure on the division-leading Brewers, who led by only 1½ games despite surging to a 54-36 record, a season-high 18 games over .500. The first-half schedule would conclude with a road swing through Miami and Pittsburgh, with three games against the rebuilding Marlins and five games in four days against the Pirates, including a makeup doubleheader resulting from an earlier rainout at PNC Park. That trip would conclude a grueling stretch of 21 games in 20 days, with no days off.

The Brewers could have, and probably should have swept the three games in Miami. But twice they did something uncharacteristic in this season, losing in the late innings. Extra innings, as a matter of fact. In the opener, manager Craig Counsell handed a 2-1 lead to dominant reliever Josh Hader in the seventh inning, a formula that had worked time after time in the first three months of the season.

Hader soon found himself in a prolonged battle with Miami's Starlin Castro, who fouled off pitch after pitch to keep his at-bat alive. The Brewers thought Hader's 10th pitch was strike three but home plate umpire Brian Gorman called it ball three instead. Given that reprieve, Castro hammered the next pitch, a 93-mph fastball, out to left-center for a game-tying home run.

Stunned by that turn of events, Hader put a first-pitch fastball in a bad place to the next hitter, Brian Anderson, who crushed it out to center to give the Marlins a 3-2 lead. How shocking were those back-to-back home runs? The two homers matched the total against Hader for the entire season.

When you're as dominant as Hader, who seemingly could strike out hitters at will, it's stunning when the ball leaves the park, much less twice on two pitches. Always the same in the clubhouse afterward, be it a good outing or the occasional poor one, Hader would said, "It's baseball. I wish I could be perfect every single time I step on the mound. But, realistically, I can't."

The Brewers tied the game in the eighth inning on a run-scoring single by Travis Shaw and appeared primed to win it in the ninth when they put runners on second and third with no outs. Jesús Aguilar, who knocked in 70 runs before the break en route to an All-Star nod, failed this time, striking out against hard-throwing reliever Kyle Barraclough. Brad Miller then bounced into a double play and that was the end of that threat.

In an attempt to get some offense out of the second base position, general manager David Stearns traded power-hitting first baseman Ji-Man Choi to Tampa Bay on June 10 for Miller, a former starting shortstop no longer in favor with the Rays. Stearns and Counsell stuck with Jonathan Villar after a disappointing showing in 2017 but the mistake-prone infielder again played his way onto the bench with scant production.

Utility player Hernán Pérez was given some starts at second but Counsell preferred using him in a variety of roles off the bench. Eric Sogard, who looked like Pete Rose for six weeks with a barrage of hits in 2017, couldn't buy one this time around, batting a horrendous .134, and eventually was sent out. The position would remain a problem area until the Brewers found a unique solution at the trade deadline, acquiring Kansas City third baseman Mike Moustakas and moving Shaw to second.

As so often happens when you fritter away a prime scoring opportunity, the Brewers dropped the series opener in Miami on a run-scoring single off Corey

Knebel by backup catcher Bryan Holaday, who was playing only because starter J.T. Realmuto was on paternity leave.

"We had opportunities and we didn't do enough to win the game," said Counsell, bottom-lining the night's proceedings. "We didn't make plays we had to. We haven't had a game like that in a while."

The Brewers would have another like it two nights later, blowing their chance to win the series after pulling away to an 8-4 victory in the second game. They lost in walk-off fashion for the second time in three games to the lowly Marlins, with Castro knocking in the winner in the 12th inning off rookie Jorge Lopez, pressed into extended action with few arms available in a weary bullpen.

The last thing the Brewers needed in a night getaway game was a 12-inning marathon, guaranteeing their charter flight to Pittsburgh would not land until the wee hours of the morning. The Brewers were playing for the 16th consecutive day and still faced the five-game, four-day series in Pittsburgh.

"We're in the middle of a pretty long stretch right here," Shaw said before boarding the late flight. "We're not going to win every series. We'll just try to finish up strong in this next series before the break."

The Brewers seldom looked forward to trips to Pittsburgh. Nothing against that fine city but it always seemed to rain there, as it did during the first series in June, necessitating the makeup doubleheader on the Saturday before the break, yet another game added to the 20-day gauntlet to close the first half.

Beyond the need to pack rain gear, the Brewers generally did not fare well at PNC Park, whether the Pirates were good, bad or in-between, as they appeared to be in 2018. The ballpark on the banks of the Allegheny River opened in 2001, the same year that Miller Park debuted, and fans loved it for its scenic panorama of the downtown Pittsburgh skyline.

The Brewers were not there for the scenery, however.

Milwaukee lost the first six games it played at PNC park in '01 and went 1-9 there during that inaugural season. It hadn't gone much better in the interim, with only 64 victories in 148 games. The Brewers stumbled to a 3-7 record there in 2017, when they fell one victory short of the NL's second Wild Card playoff berth.

This series would result in a new level of misery. The Brewers looked like a tired team in the opener, not too surprising considering they didn't get to their hotel until 5 a.m. after traveling all night from Miami. Those who fly commercial aviation are never going to feel sorry for well-paid players who travel on chartered jets with free food, but a team needs a day off every now and then and the Brewers couldn't remember their last one.

Showing little offensive life until scoring twice in the ninth, the Brewers bowed meekly, 6-3, with light-hitting Pirates shortstop Jody Mercer driving in four runs. The only good news was the return of left-hander Wade Miley, who had recovered from a two-month stay on the disabled list with an oblique strain.

There was an uplifting moment for the team afterward when it was announced that reliever Jeremy Jeffress was added to the NL All-Star team, replacing injured Washington reliever Sean Doolittle. The 30-year-old Jeffress had battled many demons in keeping his career alive, a back story which his teammates were fully aware, leading to an emotional celebration.

"We had a great reaction from the team," Counsell said. "They were fired up for him. He was fired up. He is deserving. I told him today, 'You're getting better. I feel like you've become a better pitcher.'"

It was back to reality the next day, a 7-3 thumping that looked much like the previous night. It was ugly from the very start, with the Pirates scoring three runs in the first off Junior Guerra, who showed up with no command of his pitches. The offense again was flat, offering little resistance against rookie starter Nick Kingham, who entered with a 3-4 record and 4.26 ERA.

His team's gas tank was sitting on empty but Counsell was not one for making excuses. Asked if his team looked weary to him, he replied tersely, "We're 90 games in. We've got 70 games to go. It's not time to be tired."

The offense remained MIA the next day, scoring a mere three runs over 18 innings as the Pirates' underrated pitching staff refused to let the Brewers up for air in a doubleheader sweep. It was the longest day of the season in so many ways, and only got uglier in the eighth inning of the nightcap when the Pirates belted three home runs off reliever Aaron Wilkerson, added as a 26th player from the minors as rules allowed for doubleheaders.

The Brewers scored only one run through 17 innings before Aguilar singled in two runs in the ninth of Game 2. In the opener, Chase Anderson allowed two first-inning homers, continuing a season-long trend that he'd never shake. The shots by Starling Marte and Gregory Polanco were Nos. 18 and 19, compared to the 14 that Anderson surrendered in the entire 2017 season.

"For the last two years, we've had trouble scoring runs in this park, it feels like to me," Counsell said, and he was right on the money. Going back to the previous season, the Brewers had gone 4-12 at PNC Park, scoring a total of 36 runs, an average of 2.25 per game.

The first half proved to be a week too long for the Brewers, who had one last chance in the series finale to salvage one victory and avoid a six-game losing streak entering the All-Star break. Instead, they would suffer their most crushing loss of the season, considering the circumstances.

The offense finally showed up in that fifth game, or to be more specific, Brett Phillips showed up. The rookie outfielder was called up from Class AAA Colorado Springs to provide another bat and delivered a three-run triple in the eighth and go-ahead, run-scoring single in the 10th. Had the Brewers' usually dependable bullpen done its part, the losing streak would have ended.

Jeffress gave one run back in the eighth but all Knebel had to do was protect a two-run lead in the ninth and the Brewers would be winners. After loading the bases with no outs by walking Max Moroff, a .185 hitter, Knebel had a chance to escape when Mercer grounded into a double play. Instead, he allowed a game-tying triple to David Freese, a longtime Brewers nemesis dating to his days with St. Louis.

When Phillips came through again in the 10th, the bullpen had another chance to save the day. Taylor Williams looked to be the man to do it but with two outs and a runner on, and left-handed hitting Colin Moran due up, Counsell lifted the young righty in favor of lefty specialist Dan Jennings.

This was how Counsell operated his bullpen all season, going with match-ups and pulling relievers, whether throwing the ball well or not. Moran was batting .162 against lefties and Williams was far more effective against right-handed hitters, so the Brewers' manager considered it a no-brainer.

"Moran rarely hits against left-handers, actually," Counsell explained.

But another factor came into play during the pitching change that could not be ignored. As Jennings trotted in from the bullpen beyond center field and made his warm-up tosses, the skies opened and it began raining hard. Very hard. With two outs in the bottom of the 10th and players on both teams looking to make flights home for the break, the umpires allowed play to continue, which was both understandable and absurd.

Unable to get a good grip on the baseball, Jennings allowed an opposite-field single to left by Moran, negating the matchup Counsell had sought. Switch-hitting Josh Bell, batting right-handed, sent a drive through the rain and over the head of center fielder Lorenzo Cain for a game-winning, two-run triple. The relay home was in time to get Moran but skidded past catcher Erik Kratz, a fitting end to what became a complete debacle.

As players hurriedly dressed in the visiting clubhouse to try to make their flights, a dazed Counsell sat in the manager's office, trying to make sense of what just happened, and how such an otherwise uplifting first half ended with a 1-7 trip and six consecutive losses.

"This one stings today," Counsell said, carefully measuring his words. "It's going to sting on the flight home. It's the kind of loss that stays with you a little bit."

No team needed the four-day break more than the Brewers, who despite improved depth were not up to playing 21 games over 20 consecutive days. The disastrous final week dropped them from 1½ games up in the NL Central to 2½ games behind the Cubs.

"The break will do everybody a lot of good," Jeffress conceded. "We need a mental and physical break."

CHAPTER NINE

You can't escape your past

There's nothing quite like your first All-Star Game, particularly if you're a young player just getting your career going. Such was the case for Josh Hader, the Brewers' dominant strikeout sensation who was an easy choice for the National League bullpen. In his first full season in the majors, Hader headed with teammates Jeremy Jeffress, Lorenzo Cain, Christian Yelich and Jesús Aguilar for Washington, D.C., where the midsummer classic would be held at Nationals Park.

It was a dream come true for Hader, in large part because the game would be played a short drive from his home in Millersville, Md., making it easy for family and friends to attend. There was no way to know if he'd see action out of a talent-laden bullpen but Hader had every intention of soaking up the atmosphere and enjoying every minute of his first All-Star experience.

"It's definitely special," Hader said after being informed he made the NL staff. "Last year, I was able to play in front of my family and friends in D.C. (during a series against the Nationals) but to go back there for the All-Star Game, words just really can't describe it."

Hader had every reason to expect the experience to be the highlight of his professional career, if not his life. Instead, it became a total nightmare, all because of something stupid he did many years earlier as a teenager.

Summoned to pitch in the eighth inning, Hader surrendered a three-run home run by Seattle's Jean Segura that snapped a 2-2 tie. He would be spared the loss when the NL rallied to erase that deficit but he wouldn't be spared public humiliation and denigration when someone posted vile, vulgar messages from Hader's Twitter account.

The tweets had been posted by Hader as a teenager in 2011 and 2012, before he became a professional baseball player. Many appeared to come from musical lyrics and included homophobic, misogynist and racial slurs, including the N-word. The firestorm that followed was quick and wide-spread on social media.

Hader was informed of the situation as he came off the field, and his Twitter account was quickly locked from public view. He could have avoided reporters by hiding in a backroom of the NL clubhouse but came out to his locker to take questions from reporters.

Hader, then 24, tried to explain the tweets were a sign of immaturity as a teenager. "I was young, immature and stupid," he said. "There's no excuses for what was said."

Asked for the context of those tweets, Hader said, "It was something that happened when I was 17 years old, and as a child I was immature and obviously did some things that were inexcusable. That doesn't reflect on who I am as a person today."

Such explanations will only get you so far. Hader would learn that members of his family had to remove the All-Star replica jerseys they were wearing in the stands with his name on them because of backlash from spectators who read the horrific tweets on their mobile phones.

It was evident that this controversy was not going to go away even though Cain, an African American, tried to defuse it somewhat by telling reporters in the clubhouse, "I know Hader. He's a great guy. I know he's a great teammate. We all say some crazy stuff when we're young.

"I'm fine. Everybody will be OK. We'll move on from it."

There would be necessary steps to take before Hader would be allowed to move on, however. The Brewers and Major League Baseball were heard from the next morning. There was nothing in the Collective Bargaining Agreement that allowed him to be fined or suspended but MLB decreed that Hader would go through sensitivity training and participate in diversity initiatives.

General manager David Stearns released a statement that condemned Hader's tweets as "inexcusable, and he is taking full responsibility for the consequences of his actions. In no way do these sentiments reflect the views of the Brewers organization or our community."

What made the situation difficult to process for teammates, staff, front office members, and for that matter, reporters, was that the soft-spoken Hader was the last person on the team you'd expect to publicly make such vile comments, no matter his age at the time. He was polite, always willing to please, never a braggard or loudmouth, and by all appearances, a person of high character.

How was one to reconcile Hader's current conduct with those terrible tweets from his youth?

"Those of us that have come to know Josh do not believe that these posts are representative of his beliefs," Stearns said in his statement. "He has been a good teammate and contributor to the team in every way."

The next day, the Brewers held a voluntary workout at Miller Park in preparation for the second half of the season. Hader was not present but that was because manager Craig Counsell allowed All-Stars to sit out the workout to get some rest after the hectic few days.

That left Hader's teammates to answer questions from a media horde that came to the ballpark for one reason: to get reaction about the pitcher's youthful yet inexcusable mistakes. The general sentiment in the clubhouse was one of forgiveness but there also was a sense of disbelief that such comments could have been attributed to Hader, even as a teenager.

"I'm disappointed," Counsell said. "At the same time, I'm confused because it's not the person or the teammate that I've known the last three years (including time in spring training). That's how I think a lot of guys feel."

Ryan Braun, the senior member of the club in terms of service, was quick to call Hader's comments "unacceptable." But he added, "In my experience of knowing him, I've never see him act that way or speak that way, or do anything remotely like that."

No one in the Brewers' clubhouse was more qualified to comment on Hader as both a person and teammate than young outfielder Brett Phillips. The two had been roommates for three years, at Class AA Biloxi, Class AAA Colorado Springs and with the Brewers. You really get to know a person when you live with them, and Phillips assured reporters that Hader in no way resembled the thoughts he posted as a teenager.

Known inside and outside the clubhouse for his hilarious, wind-sucking laugh, Phillips was dead serious when he said, "I've lived with Hader the last three years. I'm a Christian man and not once has he made me feel uncomfortable. Not once has he made me feel as if he is a racist or someone who talks down to women. He's a great teammate and that's who he's been since I've known him.

"I didn't know Hader back in 2011. It sounds like he was in a dark place and just not a good person. But that's not who he is now. I'm here to tell you he's one of my best friends in baseball and out of baseball, and that's not who he is anymore. I'm a firm believer that people can change for the good or bad, and seeing those tweets, he has changed for the best."

The timing of the controversy couldn't have been worse for the Brewers, who staggered into the break with six consecutive losses. Then came the news that Baltimore third baseman/shortstop Manny Machado, whom they had tried to acquire in trade, instead was dealt to the Los Angeles Dodgers, who just happened to be coming to Miller Park to open the second half. What next?

"There's a lot of different ways this could go, a lot of directions this could go," said third baseman Travis Shaw, a quiet leader who spoke softly but carried a lot of weight in the clubhouse. "It's not something that a week later everybody is going to forget about. It's something we're going to have to manage and he's going to have to manage."

The next day, the Brewers held the most important clubhouse meeting of the season. This was the kind of thing that could fracture team chemistry if not handled properly by the protagonist, but Hader hit every note exactly right in a tearful apology to his teammates.

Hader tried to explain the mistakes he made in his youth and begged for forgiveness. More important, he apologized to his teammates for putting them in the uncomfortable position of having to answer questions about it. Had Hader done anything in the past to irk or disgust teammates, the apology would have rung false. But he had comported himself in humble, classy fashion, so there was little or no pushback.

"I think it was a good meeting," said outfielder Christian Yelich. "A lot of things that needed to be said, needed to be covered, were touched on. We all got on the same page as far as how everybody is feeling and what we can do as a team moving forward."

After that session, Hader met with members of the media in the Miller Park interview room. As he stood, surrounded by cameras and microphones, several teammates filed into the room and gathered behind the pack in a show of support.

Asked what it meant for teammates literally to have his back, a tearful Hader said, "It's amazing. It tells me we are a true family. This is a distraction they shouldn't have to worry about. I'm grateful for having my teammates behind me and supporting me. I hope they know the person I truly am."

Watching that scene unfold was Billy Bean, MLB's first ambassador for inclusion and now a vice president and special assistant to Commissioner Rob Manfred. Bean, who came out as gay after retiring as a player, knew the possible powder keg that existed if not handled in the right way by Hader and the team. He had come to begin the mandated sensitivity training and after a two-hour meeting with Hader, was convinced that Hader was truly remorseful and no longer representative of those vulgar thoughts as a teenager.

Bean had watched how Hader handled himself in the moments after the controversy exploded on social media in Washington, and liked that initial interaction. The meeting with Hader reinforced his opinion that Hader could move past the ugly episode, and Bean was truly impressed by the outward show of support from teammates.

"I had a really strong instinct that I would find what I did find today," Bean said of the manner in which Hader conducted himself in the worst moment of his life.

After the clubhouse meeting, Counsell encouraged his players to meet privately with Hader if they had further questions. The healing process had begun, and the manager knew it would continue for some time. But Counsell had seen the chemistry grow in his tight-knit clubhouse and was confident his players would remain united.

"Frankly, I'm impressed and proud with how empathetic they've been," Counsell said. "How they've understood that whatever caused this a long time ago to happen, that in a lot of ways, they're the reason that Josh has become the person he's become, and baseball is the reason that Josh has become the person that we're all proud to call a teammate and a friend, a good, contributing member of us and society, and Milwaukee and this state."

There was one last test Hader had to pass to have any chance of moving past this ugly episode. How would the fans react the next time he took the mound at Miller Park? Hader stayed in the bullpen as the Brewers opened the second half with a 6-4 loss to the Dodgers, extending their losing streak to seven games.

The next night, with the Brewers holding a 4-2 lead in the seventh inning, Counsell summoned Hader as he had in such situations throughout the season. Admittedly nervous about what reception awaited him, Hader was blown away, beyond all expectations, upon receiving a standing ovation from the home crowd as he trotted in from the bullpen.

Back doing what he did best – blowing fastballs past hitters – Hader pitched a scoreless seventh inning and struck out the side in the eighth. Corey Knebel put the Dodgers to bed in the ninth and the toughest week of the season ended on a positive note. The losing streak was kaput, Hader experienced the forgiveness of home fans and the Brewers finally could look ahead, not behind them.

Some media outlets reported the standing ovation from Brewers fans was an endorsement of Hader's misguided beliefs as a teenager, an interpretation that totally missed the point. The home fans were not signing off on vile thoughts. They were applauding Hader for how he handled himself in the days afterward, with reinforcement from the manner in which teammates reacted and supported him.

"I'm focusing on my job and not letting anything from the past haunt me, and not be a distraction," Hader said after the Brewers finally were able to exhale as an organization. "This is what I love to do. It helps clear my mind."

As for the loving response of the home fans, Hader added, "That means a lot, having the Milwaukee support and knowing they know my true character, and forgiving me for my past. That's not who I am today."

There was a valuable lesson for all young people who don't think before using social media as an outlet for expressions, good or bad. That stuff doesn't really go away, so never believe you're totally in the clear. At the worst possible moment, when you're experiencing what otherwise would be a glorious occasion, you can be brought crashing back to earth. Be careful. Someone is always watching.

CHAPTER TEN
Let's have some fun

For those who hadn't paid attention, the Josh Hader incident provided proof of just how close the Brewers players had become, and how they had each other's backs when it counted most. During a rebuilding process that was trying at times, manager Craig Counsell repeatedly encouraged his players to "stay connected."

Counsell played for 15 years in the majors, including being part of World Series championship teams in Miami in 1997 and Arizona in 2001. He understood that on-field success usually was linked to off-field chemistry, and the ability of players to look past their own noses and support their teammates.

General manager David Stearns and his staff did background checks on every player they considered acquiring to gauge character in addition to their baseball talents. The rebuilding Brewers were willing to take chances on players roadblocked in other organizations, and many came with riveting personal stories of what it took to keep plugging away when things looked bleak.

Those players knew it took opportunity to prove they could play, and when provided one by the Brewers, were grateful to finally get a chance. That dynamic tended to create a bond among players, who came to understand the benefits of an all-for-one, one-for-all approach.

In the Brewers' clubhouse, an unanticipated benefit developed from the growing contingent of Hispanic players as Stearns rebuilt the roster. If you've ever been to a winter ball game in the Dominican Republic, Puerto Rico or Venezuela, you know the atmosphere is, shall we say, a bit "looser" there. That extends to the field, where players are more apt to do bat flips and pitchers

Home run celebrations became like Mardi Gras in the Brewers dugout. Here teammates toss confetti to celebrate a Christian Yelich home run.
AP PHOTO

perform gyrations on the mound than their American counterparts, who often are afraid of breaking the unwritten rules of comportment.

Because many of the Hispanic players on the Brewers' roster played against each other in their native countries as well as the minor leagues, they were well acquainted. By all appearances, they liked each other and had fun together, be it kidding around in the clubhouse or celebrating accomplishments on the diamond.

Accordingly, a lot of the "juice" on the team came from that group. It's not every clubhouse where the Hispanic players set the tone for the gringos but that's the way it shook out over time with the Brewers. It was an interesting dynamic, and soon extended to dugout celebrations after home runs.

Beyond the usual high-fives and pats on the butt a hitter received upon returning to the Milwaukee dugout after going deep, there was a receiving line to navigate at the far end of the bench. The celebrant was required to give forearm bashes to each teammate in the gauntlet, working his way toward a television camera at the end, where mugging and/or muscle flexing usually took place.

The dugout fun was not confined to forearm bashes, however. At times, players had their own band playing as they prepared to take the field. Left-hander Brent Suter, the most animated, fun-loving player on the club, would bring a bongo set from the clubhouse to get a beat going. Utility player Hernán Pérez, catcher Manny Piña and pitcher Junior Guerra joined in with other instruments, including tambourines.

To the delight of teammates, Suter often would bang hard on his bongo set next to Lorenzo Cain, the quiet, understated center fielder who preferred a more subdued form of game preparation. Suter's goal was to get the deadpan Cain to crack a smile. Cain would stare at him with complete disdain, refusing to give in. And so it went, day after day.

Not that Cain was above having some fun with teammates while on the field. Nearly every time he delivered a big hit, and some not so big, he would turn and look at players in the dugout, raise both arms, flash a big smile and gesture with his hands and fingers until those leaning against the railing responded in kind.

Cain later explained he was requesting his teammates to "show me some love." Cain had started the gimmick while playing in Kansas City, and when both teammates and fans alike got into the act, he kept it going. Many players throughout the league had various ways to elicit responses from those in the dugouts after delivering a big hit, and this was Cain's schtick.

"Anytime a player, pitcher, anybody does something special – get a hit, hit a home run, make a diving catch – it's just letting his teammates know and the fans know to show him some love," Cain explained to Milwaukee Journal Sentinel baseball writer Todd Rosiak. "Let the love just rain down on 'em."

Lorenzo Cain asks for some love from the fans and his teammates after hitting a double against the Chicago Cubs.
AP PHOTO

Cain first started asking for the love of his new teammates in the opening series in San Diego, when he tormented the Padres by reaching base nine times in 15 plate appearances. It soon caught on and others began following suit when they reached base.

"Everybody has their own thing that they do," Cain said. "Look around and it's big in every dugout. Every team comes up with something that gets them going, gets everybody involved. It's a long season, so you find ways to have run with a lot of the stuff you do inside the clubhouse and out on the field."

Once a group is identified as a fun-loving bunch willing to do just about anything to enjoy each other's company, the sky is the limit. Caitlin Moyer, the club's director of new media, and her team constantly looked for ways to show the world the outgoing personalities of the players and came up with a brilliant idea while the Brewers were in spring training in Phoenix.

It was the 25 th anniversary of the cult baseball movie "The Sandlot," a coming-of-age tale set in 1962. The story centers on fifth-grader Scotty Smalls, who moves into a new town with no apparent baseball skills. The neighborhood kids invite him to play on a nearby sandlot field, setting the stage for a magical summer in which the youngsters bond. The key scene in the movie comes when the one baseball the boys have left is knocked over the fence and into the yard of "The Beast," a ferocious dog who everyone in the neighborhood fears. Smalls attempts to retrieve the ball but is stopped by his new friends, afraid he will be devoured.

That is the scene Moyer wanted to recreate using Brewers players dressed like the young boys in the movie. Each player was given his lines and filming began on a back field at Maryvale Baseball Park. Christian Yelich, brand new to the team, joined a cast that included Brett Phillips, Eric Sogard, Jeremy Jeffress, Josh Hader, Hernán Pérez, Chase Anderson, Jett Bandy and veteran Stephen Vogt.

The casting proved to be pure genius. Vogt was perfect as "Ham" Porter, the big kid who knocked the ball over the fence. Jeffress played the pitcher, Kenny DeNunez, who delivered the gopher ball, going as far as wearing his Negro Leagues replica cap of the Milwaukee Bears that his mother sent from Virginia.

Phillips, the Brewers' version of the class clown, always laughing and in the middle of the fun, was perfect as Smalls, who dared think about retrieving the ball. And Yelich, perhaps in a bit of foreshadowing of his season to come, was perfect as Benny "The Jet" Rodriguez, the MVP of the sandlot squad.

The best casting, which led to the punchline of the video, did not involve a human, however. Playing "The Beast" was the antithesis of a snarling, scary canine, "Hank the Ballpark Pup."

Hank was the smallish fluffball of a dog who became the team mascot after being found as a stray at Maryvale Baseball Park in February 2014 by third base coach Ed Sedar. Hank eventually was taken to Milwaukee, where he became the darling of the town, leading to unforeseen marketing opportunities for the Brewers.

Hank had been adopted by Brewers general counsel Marti Wronski and her family, and returned to spring training to star in the final scene of the video, which became a viral sensation on social media and garnered nationwide attention. You could see how much fun the players had filming the scene, which gave folks a glimpse into the togetherness that made the '18 Brewers a special group.

It would not be easy to top "The Sandlot" video but the Brewers marketing team gave it a good shot later in the season by recreating a classic scene from another 1990s cult comedy movie, "Dumb and Dumber." In the movie, Jim Carrey's Lloyd and Jeff Daniels' Harry pick up a hitchhiker and proceed to annoy him in their own special, agonizing way.

In the Brewers' version, Suter played Lloyd and Jeffress was Harry, who were riding down the first-base foul line, not in a ratty van as in the movie, but in an old Milwaukee bullpen car that hadn't been used for decades. The video was tied to an upcoming promotion in which fans would be given a mini replica of the bullpen car before a game at Miller Park against Philadelphia.

The hitchhiker would be played by Hader, who was in need of a ride to the bullpen. Suter and Jeffress proceed to torment Hader with the childish nonsense that made Carrey and Daniels two of the most annoying characters ever to grace the silver screen. Suter steals the show with his hilarious impression of Lloyd, complete with the gap between his two front teeth.

Suter was so spot-on, in fact, that Carrey viewed it and posted his congratulations on Twitter, saying he was "tickled stupid." Carrey's message concluded with the message: "Spank You Kindly, guys!"

Over the moon that Carrey bothered to respond to the Brewers' spoof, Suter went around the clubhouse, showing the tweet to teammates. With this group, you never knew what was coming next. But you could guarantee they'd have fun doing it.

And baseball is supposed to be fun, right?

CHAPTER ELEVEN

From prospect to suspect

By the beginning of the 2016 season, Orlando Arcia was recognized as the consensus No. 1 prospect in the Brewers' farm system. Thus, it was no surprise when he was called up with two months remaining in the season and installed as the starting shortstop, with expectations of being one of the foundations of the team's large-scale rebuilding process.

Arcia didn't do much offensively over those final two months but it was evident from the outset that his defensive skills made him special in the field. He would not have to be Mike Trout at the plate to be an asset because saving runs had become more valued in the modern era of analytics, and Arcia's range, arm and instincts allowed him to constantly take runs off the board for opponents. During one stretch in '17, he went 42 consecutive games without an error, the second-longest streak by a shortstop in franchise history.

Arcia gave indication during the 2017 season that he could be an offensive asset as well. After a very slow start that made some wonder if the final two months of '16 were a preview of coming attractions, he caught fire at the plate, showing power that was unexpected. With a strong push down the stretch, Arcia finished with a .277 batting average, 15 home runs, 53 RBI and 14 stolen bases in 115 games.

Had the 23-year-old Arcia merely replicated those numbers in 2018, there would have been no complaints from his bosses. Instead, he got off to a brutal start at the plate in the first month, batting .190 with a .227 OBP and .513 OPS. As often happens with young players, he started to press and only dug the hole deeper, losing confidence in the process.

Shortstop Orlando Arcia overcame a couple of stints at Class AAA Colorado Springs during the year to return and be a key part of the Brewers playoff run.
AP PHOTO

Arcia always had been a free swinger, showing little inclination to work the count. Even while producing decent results in '17, he drew only 36 walks in 548 plate appearances, resulting in a modest .324 on-base percentage. The hope was that as he matured and got more games under his belt, his plate discipline would improve and his OBP creep upward.

The month of May was only slightly kinder to Arcia. He batted .214 over 20 games with a .254 OBP and .522 OPS. Unlike the previous season, when he produced 34 extra-base hits, he was not driving the ball at all. Too many at-bats were resulting in weak grounders or pop-ups. Of his 12 hits during the month, only three went for extra bases, and nothing better than a double.

This no longer was merely a bad start. Pressing even more to get going, Arcia got into more bad habits at the plate, in particular a backward kick with his right leg that left him completely out of balance in the box. It was painful to watch at times, as Arcia gave away at-bat after at-bat, waving at pitches out of the strike zone in a desperate attempt to get going.

General manager David Stearns and manager Craig Counsell knew this could not continue. Arcia was a mess at the plate, and it was taking a mental toll. Even the most experienced of hitters loses some confidence during a prolonged slump but the effect on young players usually is more profound.

On May 25, before a home game against the Mets, the Brewers made the inevitable announcement that Arcia was being optioned to Class AAA Colorado Springs. His slump had degenerated to the point where he had two hits in his last 29 at-bats, with a current 0-for-15 skid. Overall, Arcia was batting .194 with two homers and 13 RBI.

Arcia did contribute a pair of game-winning singles – one in the 12th inning on Opening Day in San Diego and the other a walk-off hit that beat the Cubs on April 6 at Miller Park. But that wasn't enough. With catcher Manny Piña also off to a slow start at the plate, and Piña and Arcia normally batting ahead of the pitcher, the bottom third of the batting order had become something of a black hole.

There were no quarrels with Arcia's always superb defense. He already had been credited with nine defensive runs saved, tops among all major-league shortstops. But the team needed some offense from him as well, though batting in front of the pitcher was a tough assignment for a young hitter with little or no plate discipline.

The move was not made to punish Arcia. Rather, Stearns and Counsell hoped to take some of the pressure off the young player, allow him to relax and exhale. They knew there would be disappointment but that was a secondary concern at this point. And it didn't hurt that Arcia would be going to the hitter-friendly environment in Colorado Springs, where the high elevation allowed balls to travel great distances when struck well.

It was a somber day in the Brewers' clubhouse. The energetic, fun-loving Arcia was one of the more popular players among his teammates, in particularly the sizable Hispanic contingent who looked at him as a younger brother. Arcia played the game with a joie de vivre, featuring a bubbly personality that made him instantly likeable.

"We're a better team when Orlando Arcia is up here playing like we know Orlando Arcia can play," said Stearns, meeting with reporters in the dugout before batting practice. "This is an effort to help him maybe take a little bit of the pressure off, get him out of the spotlight of a major-league stadium every night and get back to being a player who can contribute offensively."

Counsell, who employed one of the more unique batting stances in the game during his playing days, understood the challenge of producing in the big leagues, particularly with so little experience. He echoed Stearns' comments that the move would be best for Arcia at that particular point in time.

"The game doesn't spare anyone," Counsell said. "It doesn't matter if you're labeled a top prospect. You go through a time when you struggle, and it's not fun, and it's challenging. It kind of works on you mentally, as I'm sure it has been doing to Orlando. But he'll get out of it. I think we're all confident that he'll come out of this better."

Counsell already had begun to give Tyler Saladino more starts at shortstop and announced that Saladino would become a regular at the position. Acquired earlier in the season from the Chicago White Sox in a move that garnered little attention, Saladino spent a couple of weeks at Colorado Springs before being added to the Brewers' roster.

Saladino made the decision easier to demote Arcia by swinging a hot bat when given a chance to play. In just over two weeks with the Brewers, he was batting .400 with three home runs and six RBI.

"Tyler's earned some playing time, and that was part of this decision," Stearns confirmed. "If we're going to start playing Tyler a little bit more, that meant at-bats for Orlando were going to become a little fewer and farther between. That didn't make a ton of sense to us at this point."

You know what they say about the best-laid plans of mice and men. Four days later, Saladino badly sprained his left ankle, turning it while stepping on second base on what otherwise should have been a routine force play. He was placed on the 10-day disabled list, a cruel fate for a career backup player finally getting his chance to play regularly and producing (.324, 3 HRs, 8 RBI in 16 games).

Of the somewhat gruesome video that showed how badly he turned his ankle, which could have been much worse, Saladino said ruefully, "I've seen it once. That's enough for me. It makes it hurt more."

After playing only four games with Colorado Springs, Arcia was recalled by the Brewers. His second chance had come much sooner than expected, and out of necessity. And, much like the first time around in 2018, it didn't go well.

You don't fix something as broken as Arcia's hitting mechanics during 15 at-bats, which was all Arcia accumulated during his brief stay in the minors. Upon returning to Milwaukee, he was unable to make the most of his playing time in Saladino's absence, batting .203 with two walks and no extra-base hits over the next month.

On July 1, the Brewers went back to Plan B, sending Arcia back to Colorado Springs. Among players with at least 150 plate appearances, Arcia was the least productive player in the NL with a slash line of .197/.231/251. This time, he would stay down as long as it took to show some real progress.

"What we originally had planned to do, we'll make another attempt at it," Counsell said after Arcia was swapped for Sky Sox pitcher Aaron Wilkerson, providing a fresh arm for an overworked bullpen.

"Unfortunately, I feel like we've kind of failed here in just trying everything we can to (get Arcia going)."

The Brewers were in a trick box with Arcia. They needed his defense – he was by far their best infielder – and didn't want to crush his spirit with a second banishment to the minors. But it was doing no one any good for him to continue to give away at-bats with a mechanically unsound approach at the plate. Top prospect or not, the bottom line in the majors is you produce or you step aside.

"Look, we're taking a defensive hit," Counsell admitted. "Defensively, we're not going to be as good. We know how good Orlando is, and really, through all of this, he has played wonderful defense. It's been really, really good the entire season. But it's important to try and get the best Orlando Arcia."

This time, Arcia would remain with Colorado Springs for more than three weeks, finally making real progress at the plate. He hit safely in 15 of 18 games and had put together an eight-game hitting streak when the Brewers recalled him on July 26. Arcia raised his average to .341 during that stretch, showing a markedly better approach at the plate that boosted his OBP to .417.

"Look, it comes down to the most important thing for hitters, and that's their ball-strike recognition and swinging at the right pitches," Counsell said. "Orlando will have success if he's swinging at the right pitches, and he always has."

The next day, it became clearer why the Brewers needed Arcia's defense back in the major leagues. With the trade deadline approaching, they surprised the baseball world by acquiring third baseman Mike Moustakas from Kansas City for two of their better prospects, outfielder Brett Phillips and right-hander Jorge Lopez.

The Brewers already had a steady, power-hitting third baseman in Travis Shaw, who had been their cleanup hitter since being acquired before the 2017 season. What did they want with Moustakas? Stearns would reveal the somewhat stunning answer, and Arcia's infield defense would be a big part of the equation.

Shaw never had played a game at second base but had been taking ground balls during pre-game BP for several days. He and Counsell downplayed the significance of that development but that piece to the puzzle made more sense when Moustakas was acquired. Never afraid to think out of the box, Stearns said Shaw would begin seeing action in games at second, which had become a problem area after disappointing Jonathan Villar played his way out of the lineup.

The 6-4, 235-pound Shaw certainly was no Baryshnikov around the middle of the infield but Stearns explained why that would not be a deal-breaker. The Brewers employed more defensive shifts than any other team in the NL, and would count on the quickness and range of Arcia to cover for the lack thereof with Shaw.

"The truth is, with the way we move our infielders around, conventional positions don't apply to us all that much," Stearns said. "We ask a lot of our infielders, to play all over the dirt. So, Travis has played all over the dirt for the majority of this season and most of last season as well.

"There's going to be a different positional number next to his name in everyone's scorebook, going forward on most nights. But in terms of actual functions of what we're asking him to do, he's probably a little more familiar with it than we would think."

The biggest challenge for Shaw would be turning double plays, something he rarely had to worry about as a third baseman, even while playing up the middle on defensive shifts. But Stearns and Counsell figured Shaw would be good enough on most nights and would not make mistakes that cost games. If that happened, the wolves would be howling at their door.

The Brewers coveted Moustakas for several reasons. He was a key cog in the Royals making it to consecutive World Series in 2014-'15, coming up with big hits, making key plays in the field and showing true leadership skills in the clubhouse. That experience figured to translate well to the Brewers, who had similar designs on making the Fall Classic.

Moustakas also was a left-handed, fly-ball hitter, which traditionally played well at Miller Park. As Stearns put it, "We think his profile fits particularly well in our ballpark, and in our lineup. He puts a lot of balls in the air. From a balance perspective in the lineup, despite the power, he really doesn't strike out all that much. So, it's a contact-oriented approach, along with the power."

To cover themselves, a few days later the Brewers gave themselves a right-handed-hitting option by trading for Baltimore's Jonathan Schoop, an established, defensively sound second baseman. But Schoop would struggle so badly at the plate that his playing time eventually would dry up. With October baseball on the line, most days it was Moustakas at third base and Shaw at second.

As an unexpected bonus, Arcia suddenly began to hit, just in the nick of time. After showing modest improvement in August (.283 batting average, one homer, five RBI), he picked up the pace considerably in September, as the Brewers pushed toward the playoffs, batting .329 with a .360 OBP and .803 OPS. Along the way, he got continued support from his teammates, including his "big brother," Jesús Aguilar.

Yes, Orlando Arcia could hit, when he was right mentally and right mechanically. But it was a painful journey getting to that place in 2018.

CHAPTER TWELVE

Erik Kratz's 15 minutes of fame

On May 25, the day the Brewers sent Orlando Arcia to the minors the first time, the team made another roster move that didn't get much attention. They acquired catcher Erik Kratz, a 38-year-old journeyman catcher, from the New York Yankees and put him on their roster, sending offensively challenged backup Jett Bandy to the minors.

Kratz had been a professional ballplayer for 17 years but had played in only 228 games at the major-league level, only 36 since 2015. Originally drafted by Toronto in the 29th round in 2002 out of Eastern Mennonite University in Harrisonburg, Va., he bounced around from organization to organization, seeing time with the Pirates, the Phillies, the Blue Jays (the second time around), the Royals, the Phillies again, the Astros, the Pirates again, the Yankees, and now, the Brewers.

Kratz showed some pop in his bat early in his career but never hit enough to project to more than a backup catcher, with a batting average just above .200. Mostly, he played at the Class AAA level, serving as insurance for teams should a catcher get injured in the majors.

But Kratz never lost hope, and more important, never lost his spirit. He always gave the game everything he had, refusing to be cheated and have regrets later. It allowed him to keep going, making all those bus rides and early-morning flights in the minors, still excited to be wearing a baseball uniform. Kratz had played for 30 minor-league clubs, been a part of 11 organizations, yet accumulated less than five years of big-league service time.

Yet, true to form, Kratz arrived in Milwaukee with a smile on his face and a positive attitude, ready to do whatever manager Craig Counsell asked. With No. 1 catcher Manny Piña struggling for the most part offensively, Kratz began to find his name in the lineup more often, and Counsell loved the way he handled himself behind the plate, showing a knack for framing pitches and handling pitchers he was still getting to know.

Pitch framing was known in the old days as "stealing strikes." It's the subtle art of making it look as if a pitch came across the corner of the plate, even if it actually missed by an inch or two. Or three. A catcher has to learn how to stealthily move his mitt closer to the zone immediately as the ball gets there, prompting the unsuspecting umpire to call it a strike.

How important is a catcher who is adept at framing pitches? It can mean the difference between the count being 2-1 and 1-2. At 2-1, the hitter is in control and can be more selective at the plate. With a 1-2 count, the pitcher can afford to pick at the corners and make the hitter swing at his pitch, rather than giving him something good to hit.

Over the many years of practicing his craft, be it mostly at the Class AAA level, Kratz had become slick at pitch framing. Therefore, pitchers loved throwing to him. And managers loved putting him behind the plate.

"If you're my age and still getting a chance to catch, you must be doing something right," Kratz said. "I'm always trying to improve. That's the key to staying in this game. You can never be satisfied."

That doesn't mean Kratz never thought about quitting and going home to spend more time with wife Sarah and the couple's three children. He didn't get his first taste of the majors until he was 30 in July 2010 with Pittsburgh, and then for only nine games. The next year, his action in the big leagues consisted of two games with Philadelphia.

Even when Kratz caught the unexpected break to be with the Kansas City Royals when they made it to the 2014 World Series, he never got off the bench. Starter Salvador Perez played every inning of all seven games as the Royals were edged by Madison Bumgarner and the San Francisco Giants.

The Royals would return to the World Series the next year and win it but Kratz didn't even get to watch from the dugout. He suffered a foot injury early in the season, prompting the team to trade for Drew Butera. When Kratz was ready to return to action, Kansas City kept Butera and designated him for assignment.

And so it went for Kratz, who went through airports more often than flight crews. All told, he was released, granted free agency, traded or sold to another club a total of 15 times. Always the optimist, he considered it nice to be wanted.

"I always thought when I went to a new club I was there to stay," he said. "Then, it was 'see you later.' I learned to adjust."

Kratz, still a physical specimen at his age at 6-4, 250 pounds, never envisioned when the Brewers rescued him from the Yankees' Class AAA Scranton-Wilkes Barre affiliate the opportunity that awaited. Timing is everything in life, including baseball, and he arrived in Milwaukee at the perfect time to make an impact. Now, it was up to him to take advantage of it.

With an affable demeanor and a great back story catcher Erik Kratz became a fan favorite during the 2018 season.
AP PHOTO

And Kratz began doing exactly that. Slowly but surely, he began influencing games, not only with his savvy work behind the plate, which Counsell constantly complimented, but with some big hits, something unexpected from a career backup with no real offensive resume. One hit, in particular, helped the Brewers pull off one of their most improbable victories of the year, on August 24 against Pittsburgh at Miller Park.

The Brewers were one strike away from a 4-3 victory in the ninth inning when Pirates outfielder Starling Marte delivered a run-scoring single against reliever Jeremy Jeffress, who had been so effective all season at shutting down rallies. Then, as so often happens when one team rallies to tie the game in the ninth, the two offenses went into shutdown mode. It got so bad that the Brewers managed one hit from the seventh through 14th innings, a Ryan Braun single.

The last man standing in the Brewers' bullpen was swingman Jordan Lyles, a recent acquisition from San Diego. Lyles took over in the 14th and found himself in a jam not entirely of his own making the next inning. With two on and two down, Pirates catcher Francisco Cervelli blooped a single into no-man's land in shallow right. Second baseman Jonathan Schoop bobbled the ball after tracking it down, allowing both runners to score for a 6-4 lead.

Pittsburgh closer Felipe Vázquez had thrown two innings earlier, so Pirates manager Clint Hurdle called on hard-throwing but unproven Clay Holmes to try to close out the Brewers. With two on and two down, all Holmes had to do was strike out Lyles, forced to bat with manager Craig Counsell out of position players.

A .123 career hitter who was 0-for-14 for the season, Lyles was instructed by Counsell not to swing until he got two strikes on him. But Holmes couldn't throw two strikes, walking Lyles on five pitches as Hurdle watched in disbelief from the visiting dugout.

"He did a good job standing there," Counsell would quip after the 5-hour, 36-minute marathon. "That was his job, and he did it well."

That brought to the plate Kratz, who already had two hits for the night. He fell behind in the count, 1-2, before muscling a cutter that jammed him a bit to center for a two-run single that tied the game. Given that reprieve, Orlando Arcia punched a 92-mph fastball the other way and through the right side, winning the game.

Afterward, Kratz explained the key to pulling out an improbable victory, here and there.

"You've got to keep putting together good at-bats," he said. "I don't think anybody was giving away at-bats. You've just got to get the job done."

Beyond his solid work behind the plate and occasional offensive contributions, Kratz showed up in Milwaukee with a hidden talent that would prove useful. He could throw a knuckleball. Nearly every player will tell you they can throw a knuckler, and are happy to demonstrate it on the sidelines before games. But actually having one you can throw for strikes is a different matter entirely.

Of the many different ways the game is being played during the modern era of analytics, one growing trend has been the use of position players to mop up one-sided losses. The thinking is simple: Why waste an actual pitcher in a game you have no chance of winning? That's why, more and more, you see teams using position players to cover the final inning or two in blowouts.

Utility player Hernán Pérez, who had played every position in the majors except catcher, had been Counsell's go-to "pitcher" in such situations but Kratz informed him he could chip in as well. Kratz had pitched a couple of innings in 2016, one for Houston and the other for Pittsburgh. Once Counsell saw the big catcher throw a few knuckleballs, he was sold.

In a 13-3 romp over the Brewers in Cincinnati on June 30, Reds infielder Eugenio Suarez, who was leading the NL with 60 RBI, got a close-up view of Kratz's knuckler and couldn't bring himself to swing at it. Suarez took the rainbow, which looked more like an eephus pitch at 59-mph, for strike three and walked back to the dugout, shaking his head.

Asked about his outing, Kratz said, "We don't want to wear anybody else's arm out. So, if it can get some guys fresh so we can use them tomorrow or the next day, I definitely take pride in that."

Two days earlier, after a 6-4 victory over the Reds, Kratz provided one of the best quotes of the season for reporters. There had been a brief bench-clearing episode during the game, during which a frustrated Joey Votto exchanged words at the plate with Kratz.

Both players downplayed that argument but Kratz's description was priceless, with a nod to Votto's native country.

"We were discussing the Canadian dollar and flawed systems in our two governments," Kratz said with a somewhat straight face. "He was coming from a different side of it and we were just discussing those kinds of things."

In an 11-2 drubbing by the Dodgers at Miller Park in the first series coming out of the All-Star break, Counsell used Pérez for two innings and Kratz for another to finish the game. Starter Brent Suter exited early with an arm injury that would result in him undergoing Tommy John surgery, and with his team down nine runs in the fifth inning, Counsell saw no reason to use more relievers.

It was only the second time in franchise history, and first since 1979, that multiple position players pitched in the same game for the Brewers. Pérez had mixed feelings about his outing, admitting it was fun to try to get fellow hitters out but not under those circumstances.

"I don't like to pitch because when I'm pitching, we're losing," he said. "And I don't like to lose."

Kratz concurred, adding, "You don't want to be out there but there is a benefit to it later down the road. So, you've got to go out and do it and enjoy the moment. It's a necessity on days like this."

Kratz would make three mound appearances before the season was done but his biggest moments would come with the bat. He became a hitting star in the NLDS sweep of Colorado, making the most of his first postseason action. With an affable demeanor, a great back story and a lot to say, Kratz found a horde of reporters waiting for him at his locker during that series.

Kratz became the oldest player to start a game in his postseason debut since Lave Cross, who just happened to be a Milwaukee native, with the Philadelphia Athletics in 1905. After bouncing around to nearly half the organizations in baseball, Kratz finally was having his 15 minutes of fame, and he made sure to enjoy it to the fullest.

CHAPTER THIRTEEN
_____

The reinforcements arrive

During the Brewers' rebuilding process, nearly every veteran making any kind of money was dealt for younger major leaguers and/or minor-league prospects. As a result, the team payroll dropped considerably in both 2016 and 2017. The Brewers began those seasons with salaries totaling about $60 million, ranking at or near the bottom of the 30 clubs.

Brewers principal owner Mark Attanasio vowed that money would be put back in the team when it was ready to win again. The Brewers' performance on the field in '17, when they unexpectedly contended for a Wild Card playoff berth before falling one game short, proved they were ahead of schedule and ready sooner than expected.

In large part because of the acquisitions of right-hander Jhoulys Chacín and outfielders Lorenzo Cain and Christian Yelich, the payroll was bumped to about $91 million at the outset of the 2018 season, an increase of some 50%. Following his longtime practice, Attanasio promised there would be more funds available to add players before the July 31 trade deadline if the Brewers were in the thick of the playoff hunt.

Despite the final-week slide of the first half, when the Brewers went 1-7 and lost all five games in Pittsburgh, they were in definite contention, and general manager David Stearns and his staff began exploring possible trade acquisitions to bolster the team's chances. A deep and talented bullpen was the team's obvious strength but Stearns' view was that you never can have enough relief options.

With that in mind, Stearns swung a deal on July 26 with the Chicago White Sox for veteran reliever Joakim Soria. Left-hander Kodi Medeiros, the Brewers' first-round draft pick in 2014 out of high school in Hawaii, was the key piece sent to the White Sox as another experienced arm was added to the back end of the bullpen.

"This is the price of poker," Stearns said of surrendering a first-rounder. "We view Soria as one of the better available arms on the market this year and he fits our team well."

Though 34 years old, Soria was still an effective pitcher with postseason experience. He was closing games for the rebuilding White Sox, posting an impressive 2.56 ERA with 16 saves and .230 opponents batting average over 40 outings.

It was the second consecutive season Stearns pulled off a deadline deal with Chicago for a late-inning reliever. The previous July, he acquired veteran righty Anthony Swarzak, who used a wipeout slider to dominate right-handed hitters and post a 2.48 ERA over 29 outings for the Brewers.

Stearns' scouting staff saw a similar dynamic with Soria, whose strikeout rate of 11.4 per nine innings was his highest since 2009 with Kansas City. He had been particularly effective in recent weeks, with a 0.74 ERA over his last 25 appearances, and no extra-base hits allowed over 25 innings. In other words, he was on a tear.

Since closer Corey Knebel's early-season hamstring injury sidelined him for six weeks, manager Craig Counsell had eschewed using a traditional ninth-inning closer. He mixed and matched with strikeout sensation Josh Hader, escape artist Jeremy Jeffress, cold-blooded rookie Corbin Burnes and Knebel, depending greatly on pitcher/hitter matchups.

Counsell called his pitchers "out-getters" and discouraged talk of specific roles, either from his relievers or reporters covering the club. He said Soria would be added to that mix with no caveat other than being used in high-leverage situations, as he had in the past. Veteran right-hander Matt Albers, who pitched in the late innings in lights-out fashion over the first two months, fell apart afterward and later was sidetracked by injuries, and Soria would help fill that void.

Whenever an inquiring mind without that background knowledge asked about a certain reliever's role, Counsell invariably would say, "His role is to be ready to pitch and get outs," or some version thereof. End of discussion. Move along, nothing to see here.

The next day, the rival Cubs made a bigger move that would pay immediate dividends. Chicago decided to take a chance on veteran starter Cole Hamels, who was struggling badly (5-9, 4.72 ERA in 20 starts) with Texas while pulling down a $23.5 million salary. Hamels was once one of the top starters in the game and a postseason hero with Philadelphia in 2008, earning MVP honors in both the NLCS and World Series.

The Cubs considered Hamels a perfect change-of-scenery candidate, believing he would get re-focused and re-energized when thrust into a pennant race. That turned out to be an astute judgment, as the Brewers would soon learn.

But Stearns wasn't done making moves. Later that day, he pulled off a significant and surprising deal, acquiring veteran third baseman Mike Moustakas from Kansas City. Nobody saw that one coming because the Brewers already had a left-handed home-run hitter at third base in Travis Shaw. But, much like adding Soria to an already robust bullpen, Stearns considered it just as vital to build a deeper batting order.

Stearns announced the decision to move Shaw to second base, opening third for Moustakas. But he was not done making moves that seemed redundant to outsiders. Four days later, just minutes before the July 31 trade deadline expired, Stearns acquired second baseman Jonathan Schoop from Baltimore in a deal that included one of the Milwaukee's top pitching prospects, right-hander Luis Ortiz.

Also sent to the Orioles was second baseman Jonathan Villar, who went from promising breakthrough to flop, seemingly overnight. After the athletic Villar had an impressive offensive showing at shortstop in 2016, including a major-league best 62 stolen bases, he was moved to second base to make room for prospect Orlando Arcia.

Stearns thought so highly of Villar, he offered a $23 million extension the next spring to buy out his upcoming arbitration years. Villar and his agent decided that wasn't enough and decided to play out the 2017 season and take their chances in arbitration. That turned out to be a big mistake, as Villar slipped in every phase of the game, including an ongoing proclivity for making dumb mistakes on the bases.

The Brewers doubled down that spring on Villar by putting second baseman Scooter Gennett on waivers, seeking to get out from under his $2.5 million salary. The Cincinnati Reds obliged and snapped up Gennett, made him their everyday second baseman and watched him bloom into an offensive force, including a rare four-home run game in 2017.

Villar's slide continued in '18, creating a revolving door at second base. During one stretch players came and went at a dizzying pace. Eric Sogard couldn't hit his weight, which was only 180 pounds, and was shipped out. Brad Miller was acquired from Tampa Bay but struck out an alarming 31 times in 74 at-bats and also was shown the door.

No wonder the team's brain trust decided to give Shaw a look at second base. What did they have to lose? Schoop was supposed to provide right-handed balance at the position but could not get going at the plate and soon found himself watching games from the bench.

The Brewers thought Schoop would provide more pop to an already potent lineup. He struggled through the first half of the season with Baltimore but hit 32 home runs and drove in 105 runs during an All-Star season in 2017, and had begun to swing a hot bat before the trade deadline, earning AL Player of the Week honors.

But it was the first trade for the 26-year-old Schoop, and he never looked comfortable wearing a Brewers uniform. He hit a memorable game-winning grand slam off San Francisco ace Madison Bumgarner but otherwise was a non-factor, batting .202 in 46 games with a terrible .577 OPS. Sometimes, players do not adjust to a new environment, no matter how talented.

Schoop made Stearns so nervous with his poor showing that the Brewers' baseball boss opted to non-tender him after the season rather than gambling on a $10 million salary through arbitration. Stearns ran the risk of looking dumb for letting him go if Schoop went elsewhere and thrived, but small-market teams cannot write off $10 million mistakes like the big spenders in the game.

So, in what was primarily a financial decision, the Brewers cut loose Schoop, who quickly signed with Minnesota for $7.5 million. Not every general manager would take full responsibility for a trade that didn't work right away, but Stearns looked in the mirror and pointed a finger directly at himself.

"Look, I view it as a bad deal and that's on me," Stearns told reporters in a telephone call after the decision was announced to non-tender Schoop at the end of November. "We looked at our best-educated prediction going forward and the potential price tag going forward, compared with our internal alternatives and what is potentially available externally, and decided to go in this direction."

Moustakas didn't exactly tear it up at the plate but, unlike Schoop, made contributions to the team's stretch run, on and off the field. He seemed to fit in the clubhouse almost immediately, bonding with his new teammates as if he had been around for years.

Moustakas took a strange and unexpected path to Milwaukee. After setting a franchise record with 38 home runs for Kansas City in 2017, combined with 85 RBI and .835 OPS, he figured to break the bank as a 29-year-old free agent, turning down a $17.4 million qualifying offer from the Royals.

But a bull market never materialized for Moustakas, who had draft pick compensation tied to any free-agent deal. After being left in the cold all winter, he had no choice but to return to the Royals on a one-year deal for $6.5 million. It was a humbling, embarrassing experience but Moustakas kept his chin up in Kansas City, which was back in rebuilding mode after winning the 2015 World Series, until getting traded to the Brewers.

Moustakas didn't produce as he did for the Royals, batting only .256 in 54 games with a .767 OPS, eight homers and 33 RBI. But he did chip in with some big hits, including a memorable game-winner in the NLDS sweep of Colorado. And his savvy and experience made him a perfect fit in an already tight clubhouse, joining former KC teammate Lorenzo Cain in that department.

And Stearns wasn't done dealing. Though most of the trade action in the majors annually took place prior to the July 31 deadline, teams still could make deals with players who cleared waivers. The caveat was that players had to be acquired before Sept. 1 to be eligible for postseason play.

As the Brewers took the field on August 31 in Washington, D.C. to prepare to take on the disappointing Nationals, Stearns was working the phones furiously. Before the game began, the announcement came that yet another reliever had been acquired from the Chicago White Sox, left-hander Xavier Cedeno. Though considered something of a "loogie," the soft-tossing Cedeno actually fared well against right-handed hitters as well, thanks to his best pitch, a cutter.

Still, Stearns was not finished. Before the Brewers' 4-1 victory was complete, word leaked that they acquired Washington starter Gio Gonzalez, a convenient move considering the veteran lefty merely would have to switch clubhouses before the next game.

Gonzalez, 32, enjoyed some productive seasons in Washington but was having a dreadful 2018 campaign. He had been particularly awful since the All-Star break, going 1-5 with a 6.55 ERA in eight starts, including 1-4, 7.47 in six outings in August.

Stearns had tried unsuccessfully to pick up a starting pitcher before the July 31 deadline, coming close to dealing for Cincinnati's Matt Harvey. He felt compelled to add a veteran with playoff experience to his staff, and believed that Gonzalez was the perfect change-of-scenery candidate to turn things around and be a contributor.

Perhaps Stearns had a crystal ball in his office that no one knew about. Gonzalez indeed benefitted from his new surroundings, posting a 3-0 record and 2.13 ERA in five starts in September. The Brewers would win all five of those games, and as it turned out, needed every one of them.

As the clock ticked closer to midnight, Stearns still had one more move up his sleeve. While Gonzalez was answering questions from reporters in an emotional postgame press conference in the bowels of Nationals Park, word leaked that the Brewers made another trade for a seasoned veteran, acquiring outfielder Curtis Granderson from Toronto.

This is what it looks like when a team is all-in. Since late July, Stearns had picked up two relievers, Soria and Cedeño, two sluggers in Moustakas and Schoop, a starting pitcher in Gonzalez and a still productive outfielder in Granderson. With September call-ups about to arrive from Class AAA Colorado Springs, the Brewers were loaded for bear, or more specifically, Cubs.

"It's all hands on-deck for us," said assistant general manager Matt Arnold, who was traveling with the club in D.C. "That's important for us. We've got a really good team here and we want to do everything we can to help this team win all the way through September and into October."

And that's exactly what would happen.

CHAPTER FOURTEEN

Thinking out of the box

Trading for third baseman Mike Moustakas when the Brewers already had a productive player at the position in Travis Shaw was not the first time that general manager David Stearns showed a willingness to think out of the box. From his first day on the job in October 2015, Stearns was open to making any kind of move to acquire talent, always putting depth ahead of possible lineup quandaries.

The very first move by the Harvard graduate showed his willingness to consider all possibilities. He claimed right-hander Junior Guerra off waivers from the Chicago White Sox, ignoring the fact that Guerra, a converted catcher, was 30 and had pitched in a grand total of three games in the majors, all that year.

The Brewers liked how Guerra graded out in one specific rating system and also knew he was a determined player who had traveled all over the world to keep his career alive, pitching in Italy, not exactly a baseball hotbed, among other places.

Guerra rewarded Stearns' faith in him by posting a 9-3 record and 2.81 ERA in 20 starts in 2016, and has made 75 appearances for the club since being acquired.

The next off-season, Stearns again showed a knack for innovative thinking when he signed first baseman Eric Thames to a three-year, $16 million deal with a club option for 2020. Thames made no impact in his first go-round in the majors with Toronto and Seattle but went to the Korean Baseball Organization and put up fantasy-league numbers in three seasons with the NC Dinos, while also becoming a cult hero in that baseball-crazy country.

The powerfully built Thames took an immediate liking to pitching in the KBO, batting .343 in 2014 with 37 homers and 121 RBI. In three seasons with the Dinos, he hit .348 with 124 homers and 379 RBI in 388 games. Stearns didn't expect him to ravage major-league pitching in that fashion but left-handed power is left-handed power, and he figured Thames would do well at Miller Park, where the ball flies.

Stearns' expectations immediately came to fruition when Thames belted 11 home runs in April 2017, a club record for the opening month. He went on to knock 31 balls out of the park that season, tying for the team lead. Thames also showed plate discipline that Stearns' scouting staff had recommended, finishing with a respectable .357 on-base percentage.

The team co-leader in home runs that season was third baseman Travis Shaw, acquired a week after the Thames signing in a trade with Boston at the winter meetings. Shaw had been pushed aside when the Red Sox committed to free agent Pablo Sandoval at third base, and Stearns saw the opportunity to acquire a young, left-handed hitter with pop and big upside. He sent reliever Tyler Thornburg to Boston for Shaw and three minor-leaguers, including promising infield prospect Mauricio Dubon.

To say the least, Shaw's acquisition has paid off beyond all expectations. After ripping 31 home runs and leading the club with 101 RBI in 2017, he added 32 homers and 86 RBI in '18 while becoming the anchor of the batting order in the cleanup spot.

The deals kept coming as Stearns stripped the failing team he inherited and reconstructed it nearly from scratch. In January 2016, he dealt shortstop Jean Segura to Arizona and picked up starting pitcher Chase Anderson, infielder Aaron Hill and prospect Isan Diaz. Shortly afterward, outfielder Khris Davis was sent to Oakland for two prospects, catcher Jacob Nottingham and pitcher Bubba Derby.

Shortly before spring camp opened in 2017, Stearns made a seemingly innocuous waiver claim, picking up first baseman Jesús Aguilar from Cleveland. There didn't appear to be room for Aguilar on the roster but he had a sensation spring, made the club and contributed 16 homers and 52 RBI off the bench. Given the chance to play regularly in '18 when Thames was injured, Aguilar emerged as an All-Star, finishing with 35 homers and 108 RBI.

Other moves in the early stages of the process added to the talent level at the top of the organization. Infielder Jonathan Villar was acquired from Houston. Speedy center fielder Keon Broxton came in a trade with Pittsburgh. Slugging first baseman Chris Carter was signed as a free agent after the 2015 season and led the NL with 41 home runs in '16.

From the outset, Stearns knew he also had to keep a long view of the franchise. He wanted to return the Brewers to respectability as quickly as possible, but also wanted to position the team for success for years

Brewers GM David Stearns talks with team owner Mark Attanasio prior to a June 2018 game in Milwaukee. Stearns outside the box thinking has greatly increased the overall talent on the Brewers roster.
AP PHOTO

to come. At his first winter meetings in 2015, he traded veteran first baseman Adam Lind to Seattle for a trio of teenage pitchers, all just getting their careers started. One of those pitchers was Freddy Peralta, who quickly rose through the system to make his sensational debut on Mother's Day.

When Stearns was introduced as the Brewers' new general manager at the tender age of 30, one of the first questions he was asked was how long he thought it would take for the club to be good again. It was one of those trap questions that can put a new baseball boss in immediate jeopardy if he doesn't choose his words carefully.

Stearns wisely said he would not put a timetable on the team's return to competitiveness, realizing every situation is different. Small-market rebuilds can be tricky because funds are not unlimited and therefore must be used judiciously. Stearns also knew he had to simultaneously build a farm system deep enough to keep funneling talent to the top level.

Only one regular was not traded, left fielder Ryan Braun, and it wasn't because Stearns didn't try. In the run-up to the August 31 non-waiver trade deadline in 2016, the Brewers and Dodgers engaged in substantive talks for a blockbuster deal that would have involved Braun. Stearns had claimed tempestuous outfielder Yasiel Puig off revocable trade waivers from Los Angeles and used that to try to spur a trade.

Los Angeles would have run up a luxury tax bill by adding Braun's salary, so the Brewers agreed to offset it by taking pitcher Brandon McCarthy in a trade. The talks progressed to the point where Stearns told Braun to hang around the clubhouse one night late after a game in the event a deal was struck. One club source said the Brewers thought they had a deal, only to see the Dodgers call it off, supposedly with direction from ownership.

Braun had no-trade protection at the time but would have accepted a move to Los Angeles, his hometown. He had developed health issues in his 30s and was not the dynamic offensive force of a few years earlier, and still carried the stigma of a PED bust that led to a 65-

game suspension at the end of the 2013 season. Braun remained a productive player when not ailing and was signed for big money through 2020, so releasing him was not a consideration

Other than Braun and shortstop Orlando Arcia, who was developed in the Brewers' system, every position was turned over during the rebuilding process. Not every move was successful, but a large majority were, leading to a quicker-than-anticipated return to respectability.

Helping Stearns move faster through the process was the presence of manager Craig Counsell, chosen by previous general manager Doug Melvin to run the club after Ron Roenicke was fired one month into the 2015 season. Counsell and Stearns hit it off immediately, and worked in harmony to piece the puzzle back together.

In their very first meeting, Counsell said to Stearns, "We've just got to stack good decisions on top of each other. Keep stacking good decisions on top of each other, and it'll happen faster than we think."

Beyond the wise decision to tab Counsell as manager, Melvin got the rebuilding ball rolling during the 2015 season with some great trades. He acquired starting pitcher Zach Davies from Baltimore for outfielder Gerardo Parra, who was about to become a free agent. Melvin also sent center fielder Carlos Gomez and starter Mike Fiers to Houston – where Stearns was assistant GM at the time – for four prospects, outfielders Domingo Santana and Brett Phillips, left-hander Josh Hader and right-hander Adrian Houser.

Hader quickly developed into one of the most feared relievers in the National League. Santana hit 30 home runs as the regular right fielder in 2017 before backtracking. Phillips was used in the deal that acquired Moustakas for the stretch run in '18. Houser remains a pitcher to watch after being sidetracked by Tommy John surgery.

After Stearns took over for Melvin, he made transactions as if operating with a monthly quota. In his first off-season, he turned over 20 spots on the 40-man roster, a stunning overhaul of personnel. When progress on the field ensued, the pace of moves slowed down but not the scope. Stearns stunned the baseball world in

January 2018 by acquiring star outfielders Christian Yelich and Lorenzo Cain on the same day.

The deal for Yelich would not have been possible without Stearns sending catcher Jonathan Lucroy and reliever Jeremy Jeffress to the Texas Rangers before the trade deadline in 2016. In that swap, the Brewers acquired outfield prospect Lewis Brinson, who became the key player in a package of minor-leaguers sent to the Miami Marlins for Yelich.

That same winter, Stearns ignored howls from the outside world to sign either Jake Arrieta or Yu Darvish, the top free-agent pitchers on the market. Instead, he made the unheralded move of signing free agent Jhoulys Chacín, who quietly became the ace of the staff.

The Brewers defied the odds, taking less than three years to go from teardown to postseason play. Using every method of acquiring talent short of attending garage sales, Stearns kept his tunnel vision of "acquiring, developing and retaining young, controllable talent." It was more than his mantra. It was his mission.

"That was our focus on every decision," Stearns explained. "We judged every decision as to whether it forwarded that goal."

No general manager is perfect, and when you engage in transactions at this volume, there are going to be misfires. Supporting actors such as Ramon Flores, Sam Freeman, Alex Presley, Will Middlebrooks and Franklin Morales came and went. But general managers, especially young ones, cannot get gun shy. Undaunted, Stearns kept making moves, adding and subtracting players, always looking to add depth.

Team principal owner Mark Attanasio came to admire what he called an "agnostic" approach by Stearns to player acquisitions, meaning he was open-minded to anything and everything without bias or preconceived notions. In the process, the Brewers went from 73 victories in 2016 to 86 in 2017 to a pennant contender in '18.

It's one thing to move into the passing lane in a big market where money is thrown around like confetti, covering both moves that work and don't work. The margin for error is much smaller in a market such as Milwaukee, making Stearns' handiwork even more admirable.

"You put your head down and start working," Counsell said. "That's what you do. David's been nothing short of magnificent in his (first) three years here. I'm very fortunate to be able to work with him."

To get this far this quickly, you must be willing to think out of the box and take chances. Every move is not going to work. But if enough of them do, and you stay true to your process, anything is possible.

CHAPTER FIFTEEN

Yelich rides a bi-cycle

Sometimes, when a player participates in the All-Star Game, the hustle and bustle of the two days of festivities saps his energy and he returns to his team a bit drained. When Christian Yelich came back to Milwaukee after playing in the Midsummer Classic in Washington, D.C., manager Craig Counsell saw no signs of weariness. To the contrary, Yelich seemed energized, with a bit of bounce in his step.

The Brewers dropped their first game after the break to the Los Angeles Dodgers, 6-4, for their seventh consecutive loss but it certainly wasn't Yelich's fault. Ignoring the supposed lefty vs. lefty disadvantage against Dodgers starter Rich Hill, Yelich doubled in the first inning, a laser beam to deep center, lined out to deep left in the third and pounded an RBI double into the right-field corner in the fifth.

In the ninth, facing Los Angeles' star closer Kenley Jansen, Yelich tripled in a pair of runs, forcing the Dodgers to sweat out the two-run victory. His team didn't win the game, but with two doubles and a triple, Yelich was off and running in what would become a second half for the ages and the capper to one of the best seasons in franchise history.

There really is no rhyme or reason to hitting for the cycle. Collecting a single, double, triple and home run in the same game takes nearly as much luck as it does talent, and a glance through the Brewers' annals provides proof. Yes, some of the franchise's all-time greats have done it, such as Robin Yount on June 12, 1988 against the Chicago White Sox at Comiskey Park, and Paul Molitor on May 15, 1991, at Minnesota.

Christian Yelich salutes the crowd after receiving a standing ovation for hitting a triple that allowed him to complete the cycle for the second time during the 2018 season.

AP PHOTO

But some of the more obscure players to don Brewers uniforms also accomplished the feat, beginning with Mike Hegan on September 3, 1976 at Detroit. Backup catcher Chad Moeller, a career .226 hitter with 29 home runs in nearly 1,400 at-bats in the majors, became the first player in franchise history to hit for the cycle at home on April 27, 2004 against Cincinnati.

Reserve outfielder Jody Gerut, who had only 71 at-bats with the Brewers in 2010 before being released in August, hit for the cycle on May 8 of that season. Yet another backup catcher, George Kottaras, pulled off the feat on September 3, 2011 at Houston, collecting his only triple of that season and one of his five home runs.

No Brewers hitter had hit for the cycle since, a drought that was about to end in dramatic fashion, in perhaps the craziest game of the season. After dropping the opener of a three-game series in Cincinnati, 9-7, on August 28, the Brewers were in trouble again the next night, falling behind by a 10-6 score through six innings.

But Yelich would have something to say about how this game played out. A lot to say, as a matter of fact.

When Yelich stepped to the plate in the seventh inning with the Brewers trailing, 10-9, he already had two singles, a home run and double in his first four trips to the plate. A triple not only would tie the game but also give him the cycle, and Yelich obliged with a drive into the gap in right-center off reliever David Hernandez.

With the score now 11-11, a single by Yelich in the ninth off Raisel Iglesias, Cincinnati's best reliever, made him the first player since Ian Kinsler in 2009 to hit for the cycle and collect six hits in the same game. The Brewers made sure that incredible performance would not be wasted, eventually pulling out a wild 13-12 victory in 10 innings.

Asked afterward if he could remember feeling that good at the plate, Yelich reminded reporters that pre-game batting practice was washed out by rains that also delayed the first pitch by 27 minutes.

"Baseball is crazy that way," he said. "Things that you don't really expect to happen in this game happen. It was one of those nights."

Counsell was much more effusive in his praise, saying, "I've never seen a game like that. It was incredible. He's coming up there and you're thinking he can't do it again, and he does it again.

"He did everything tonight; he really did. He's driving the bus home tonight."

By that point, it was obvious that Yelich was putting together a special season, particularly since the start of the second half. The six hits boosted his batting average to .319, tops in the National League. Despite the many great hitters in franchise history, including Cecil Cooper, Yount, Molitor and Ryan Braun, the Brewers never produced a batting champion. Would Yelich be the first?

But it was more than just batting average. Yelich, whose best in four full seasons in Miami was 21 home runs in 2016, was in the midst of an impressive power surge, with seven homers in his last 10 games to give him 26 for the season.

After being traded to Milwaukee, Yelich – a predominantly groundball hitter with the Marlins – was asked if he'd try to take advantage of the hitter friendly conditions at Miller Park by changing his swing. In other words, would he join the "launch angle revolution?" No, he insisted, even as his home-run total began to climb.

"It's really hard to explain," he said with a shrug, not even trying to delve into it. "When you're this hot, you don't seek answers."

No player ever has a good explanation for being as hot as Yelich had been. Over his last 45 games, he was batting a scorching .371 with 15 home runs and 40 RBI. He was becoming much more than a threat to be the Brewers' first batting champ. Yelich now was a bona fide Most Valuable Player candidate.

And he wasn't going to cool off.

Less than three weeks later, Yelich would do the unthinkable by hitting for the cycle again. Making it even harder to believe, the feat again came against the Reds, this time in an 8-0 romp before the home fans at Miller Park.

Chants of "MVP! MVP!" had rained down from the stands in Milwaukee for some time but on this night, they were louder than ever. They reached ear-splitting

decibels in the bottom of the sixth when Yelich capped
a four-run rally by lining a two-run triple to right-
center off reliever Jesus Reyes. Afterward, Yelich would
figuratively tip his cap to veteran Curtis Granderson,
who at age 37 made the triple happen by scoring all the
way from first base, allowing Yelich to leg out the three-
bagger.

Entering 2018, there had been seven cycles in the
history of the Brewers. Now, Yelich had pulled off the
feat twice in a span of 20 days. And the second one
came the day after the runaway right fielder saw his on-
base streak snapped at 30 consecutive games in a 3-2
loss to Pittsburgh.

"The impressive thing to me is a team holds him in
check yesterday and that seems to be a bad sign the
next day for the other team," Counsell said afterward.
"Today, before the game, there was an intent that good
things were going to happen."

What did Counsell mean by that? Did Yelich have
a different "game face" on that day? Was he pacing
around the clubhouse, vowing aloud to do mean things
to the enemy pitchers? Nothing that dramatic, Counsell
explained.

"It's just competitiveness, that's all it is," he said.

Only four players in major-league history had put
together two cycles in one season, and the first two
probably rode in horse-drawn transportation to the
ballpark – Cincinnati's Long John Reilly in 1883 and St.
Louis' Tip O'Neill in 1887. Suffice it to say they were not
facing pitchers coming out of the bullpen throwing 95
mph in those days.

Informed of his rare place in the game's history, the
modest Yelich said, "It's hard to believe, hard to process.
There have been so many great players to play this
game. That just shows how freaky that is and how rare.
It's hard enough to get four hits in a major-league game,
let alone have them all be the right ones, or in the right
sequence."

By the end of the night, Yelich added five points to
his batting average, tying Reds second baseman Scooter
Gennett for the league lead at .318. Over his last 27
games, he had belted 13 home runs with 33 RBI. It was

pretty heady stuff for a young player who had batted .300 just once in Miami, hitting that mark exactly in 2015.

"It's definitely crazy," he said. "I'm trying to enjoy it as much as possible. Honestly, I don't even know how to describe it."

With the NL Central race and a playoff berth at stake, Yelich had put the team squarely on his shoulders and carried them with one big game after another. Entering September, the general feeling was that Chicago infielder Javy Baéz was the best bet for NL MVP. There were others to consider as well but Yelich was quieting all that talk, becoming the very definition of a most valuable player.

When general manager David Stearns traded for Yelich, he expected him to make a significant impact on the Brewers' lineup. But no one dreamed of anything like this, least of all Yelich. How could you? He was putting together one of the best seasons in franchise history, raising his game yet another notch when his team needed it most. And he was mostly doing it from the No. 2 spot in the batting order, not a traditional run-production spot, particularly in the NL.

As teammate Mike Moustakas put it, "What he's doing out there is pretty special. We're lucky to have a front-row seat to watch it, each and every night."

CHAPTER SIXTEEN

A Labor Day omen

As the Chicago Cubs arrived at Miller Park on Labor Day to open a three-game series against the Brewers, the two-time defending division champs had every reason to feel good about where they stood in the NL Central standings. They led second-place Milwaukee by five games, a formidable margin with less than a month left in the season.

If the Cubs took two of three from the Brewers, their lead would be all but secure. If they swept the series, the Brewers would be buried in the division race, forcing them into a Wild Card-or-bust position.

The opener was a game of twists and turns but the real drama didn't unfold until the late innings. With the Brewers holding a 2-1 lead, manager Craig Counsell pulled the plug after five innings on starter Zach Davies, who put aside an injury-plagued season for one day to shackle the Cubs on four hits while logging seven strikeouts.

Counsell summoned strikeout sensation Josh Hader, who responded with two no-hit innings, retiring all six batters he faced, to get the game to the eighth. That might be enough for some relievers, but Hader had a low pitch count and Counsell decided to give him another inning. The thinking was that Hader would need at least two days off after the outing, so why not squeeze a few more outs from him?

Hader walked leadoff hitter Ian Happ but struck out Daniel Murphy and Javier Baez, bringing to the plate Anthony Rizzo, a left-handed hitter with tremendous power. Happ stole second base on a 1-0 pitch, putting the tying run at second, but that would prove to be moot.

Hader fell behind in the count to Rizzo, 2-1, and put a fastball in a bad place. Rizzo turned on it and sent it on a towering arc to right field for a no-doubt home run that put Chicago on top, 3-2. The usual large contingent of visiting Cubs fans went nuts while Brewers fans sat in disbelief, some possibly knowing no left-handed hitter had gone deep on Hader in his year-plus in the majors.

Simply put, Rizzo beat Hader in a classic power-on-power match-up. Hader had come up and in with a fastball on the previous pitch, getting a swing and miss, and was trying to duplicate it but missed over the plate.

"I probably could have gone a little bit higher (in the strike zone)," Hader said later, analyzing the fateful pitch. "But I was trying to get inside on him and get on his hands. Professional hitter. That's the game of baseball."

It was a shocking turn of events, but the Brewers did not roll over. They put together a rally in the bottom of the inning against beanpole reliever Carl Edwards, Jr., starting with base hits by Curtis Granderson and Lorenzo Cain. Edwards struck out Christian Yelich as well as Jesús Aguilar but walked Ryan Braun on a 3-2 pitch to load the bases.

Mike Moustakas, the late-season pickup from Kansas City acquired for just these situations, came to the plate and told himself to be patient. Don't get yourself out. But Edwards made it easy on him, walking him on four pitches to tie the game.

Unhappy with the ball-strike calls by home plate umpire Gabe Morales on both Braun and Moustakas, Chicago manager Joe Maddon let him have a piece of his mind from the dugout and got ejected for his trouble. Upon being removed from the game after the walk to Moustakas, Edwards also did some barking at Morales on his way to the dugout and drew an ejection as well.

After reliever Jeremy Jeffress worked a scoreless top of the ninth, stranding the potential tying run at second base, the Brewers went to work against side-armer Steve Cishek, a nightmare for right-handed hitters because of the low, sweeping angle from which he released the ball.

Cishek began digging his own grave, walking light-hitting catcher Erik Kratz on four pitches and hitting

Orlando Arcia, mired in a season-long slump, with his first pitch. Speedy Keon Broxton ran for Kratz, and when catcher Willson Contreras, who had just come in the game, committed a passed ball, the Brewers had runners on second and third with no out.

Cishek struck out Granderson but hit yet another batter with a pitch, Cain, to load the bases. Veteran right-hander Jesse Chavez came on to face Yelich, who had been swinging the bat at a blistering pace for weeks. Behind in the count, 1-2, Yelich punched a grounder down the third-base line that Kris Bryant fielded flawlessly.

Bryant had two options and had to decide immediately which one to take. He could come home for a force at the plate, leaving the bases loaded with two down, or try for an inning-ending double play and extra innings. Bryant chose the latter, which would prove to be a bad decision, stepping on the bag at third and firing across the infield to try to nab Yelich at first.

Breaking from the left side of the box, the long-legged Yelich was hustling all the way and beat the throw by a step as Broxton scored the winning run from third. It was a walk-off fielder's choice, which felt just as satisfying to Yelich and the Brewers as if it were a grand slam.

"I saw him catch it and I saw him go to third, so I just started busting it, man," Yelich said of his sprint down the line. "You've got to find a way to get there.

"It was a lot of fun. It was a great atmosphere. Intense. All the games we play against these guys are real close."

The victory pulled the Brewers within four games of the Cubs and increased their lead over St. Louis to 1 ½ games for the first Wild Card in the NL. There were five games remaining on the schedule between Milwaukee and Chicago, and Counsell advised fans of both teams to buckle up for the ride.

"You better have a ticket because that's how the games have finished, pretty routinely," Counsell said. "It was a fun baseball game. They might not be saying the same thing, but it was a game with some great plays and a lot of individual efforts."

Momentum can be fleeting in baseball, mostly because the starting pitchers have so much say. A poor outing by your starter can take you out of the game early and kill any good feelings from the previous day. Brewers lefty Wade Miley, whose only issue all season was staying healthy, did not ruin the buzz created in the opener when he took the mound for the second game of the series.

Miley pitched six brilliant innings, allowing only three hits and one run while issuing no walks and striking out five. Watching the veteran lefty carve through the Cubs' potent batting order with his cutter and deceptive changeup made it difficult to believe it was the same pitcher who the previous September was putting a disheartening capper on the worst season of his career, going 0-5 with a 9.74 EA in his final month with Baltimore.

It was the return of Miley in mid-July from a two-month stay on the DL with an oblique injury that gave the Brewers' oft-criticized starting rotation a big boost. It was his 12th start of the truncated season and in those games Miley forged a sparkling 2.12 ERA, allowing him to form a potent righty-lefty combination with Jhoulys Chacín atop the rotation.

There had been howls from the outside world the previous offseason for general manager David Stearns to sign one of the top free-agent pitchers, Jake Arrieta or Yu Darvish. Instead, he gave Chacín a modest two-year contract before Christmas and added Miley on a non-roster deal after spring camp had begun.

"Every time we've given him the ball, Wade's done a heck of a job," Counsell said after the game. "I can't say enough about how he has pitched."

Though Stearns deserved credit for taking a chance on Miley, the player is always the one who merits the biggest pat on the back. Miley could have called it quits after his brutal 2017 season but instead went back home, reinvented himself, and was on a mission after joining the Brewers.

On this night, Miley was so precise with his pitches that his catcher, Kratz, had a grin on his face as he called for the cutter or changeup. It really didn't matter because Chicago's hitters were beating both into the ground, resulting in nine groundball outs of the 13 recorded on balls put in play.

"It's awesome to be like, 'Hmm, what should we throw? OK, we'll go with that,'" Kratz told reporters afterward. "And he has confidence in it, too, which is huge. Nobody comes in and hopes to just do a little better. You always want to come in and do a ton better."

Miley's outing was just what the Brewers needed to bide time in the game until the Cubs began self-destructing, both out of their bullpen and in the field. A modest 3-1 lead through five innings became 6-1 in the sixth, 9-1 in the seventh and, finally, 11-1 in the eighth. Chicago provided a huge helping hand by committing two errors and issuing nine walks, resulting in heavy traffic on the bases and the eventual blowout.

It was the sixth victory in seven games and the 11th in 15 games for the Brewers, who now were exerting undeniable pressure on the first-place Cubs. They were a mere three games behind, making the series finale slightly huge. Chicago would leave town with either a four-game lead or two-game lead, a significant difference with just over three weeks remaining in the season.

"Hopefully, we'll come out tomorrow and get a sweep," said a hopeful Lorenzo Cain. "We'll see what happens. We'll have to be ready to go because I know they'll be ready to go."

Unfortunately for the Brewers, Cubs left-hander José Quintana was starting the series finale, which almost always guaranteed defeat for them. Quintana wasn't completely dominating this time, as so often in the past, but was good enough, limiting the Brewers to five hits and two runs in 6 2/3 innings.

On the flip side, Milwaukee's de facto ace, Jhoulys Chacín, drove into a huge pothole in the fourth inning, surrendering four runs as Chicago snapped a scoreless tie. The rally started with a home run by Murphy and included two errors on one play on a base hit by Rizzo, allowing Baez to race around all the way from first base.

Despite Chacín's hiccup and the defensive sloppiness, the Brewers hung close enough to throw a scare into the Cubs in the bottom of the ninth. After Pedro Strop walked Travis Shaw to open the inning, Counsell sent Yelich to the plate to pinch-hit.

Knowing full-well the importance of the game, Counsell noticed Yelich had been dragging a bit and opted to give him some rest for the first time in the second half. It made common sense to manager and player, because combined with an off day on the schedule the next day, Yelich could get extra rest and recharge for the stretch run.

Because the Brewers would lose the game, 6-4, Yelich's absence from the lineup became a hot-button topic on talk radio and social media, carrying over into the team's day off and reaching a level of vitriol that surprised Counsell. The criticism also got to Yelich.

One of the most easygoing and approachable players on the team, Yelich became frustrated by what he'd heard in person while out and about on the off day as well as comments on his personal Twitter timeline. One tweet, in particular, got under his skin, from a Cubs fan who alleged Yelich asked out of the lineup to avoid facing Quintana.

"Having your competitiveness and your desire as an athlete called into question is, for sure, frustrating," Yelich told reporters when the team reported for a series against San Francisco after the off day. "The fact that it has even become something that we have to address here, I think is ridiculous, to be honest with you."

Yelich, who delivered a single in that pinch-hit appearance against the Cubs before the rally fizzled, had played in all but five innings since July 3, a span of 55 consecutive games that included nine extra-inning affairs. His 555 plate appearances led the club. In other words, he should have been able to take a game off, even an important one, without people questioning his motives.

Counsell didn't consider it a topic worthy of debate, noting he had seen signs of fatigue in the MVP candidate.

"We recognized it four days ago," Counsell explained. "We pushed it, and then it reached a point where we're not going to push this any longer, because at that point we are risking injury."

Counsell then shot a warning flare into the air, adding, "We've got some overreaction to some things going on, and that's fine. That's part of it. We're going to make our decisions here over the rest of the year, and there are going to be more difficult decisions. And you're not going to like them all."

So, the Cubs left town four games ahead of the Brewers instead of two, a big difference. The math was definitely working against the Brewers, who had 21 games remaining, compared to 23 for Chicago. By all appearances, Milwaukee's best chance to play in October was the Wild Card race.

"This was a chance to put a big dent in their division lead and we were unable to do so," Counsell said. "Now, it's on to winning games."

The Cubs had not heard the last from the Brewers.

CHAPTER SEVENTEEN

Initial 'out-getters' make early exits

It did not take a rocket scientist to figure out the
strength of the Brewers was their deep, talented bullpen.
In particular, the trio of Josh Hader, Jeremy Jeffress
and Corey Knebel was overpowering, with Knebel back
in peak form after missing time early with a hamstring
strain and scuffling with his command for periods
afterward.

With that in mind, Counsell did not hesitate to go to
his bullpen early and often throughout the season. Once
the team got to September, chasing the Cubs for the
division lead while also trying to stay atop the Wild Card
race, he figured he could make even more liberal use of
his relief corps, if that were possible.

Several factors were in play as Counsell and pitching
coach Derek Johnson plotted their course through the
September schedule. With expanded rosters for the final
month, there were plenty of extra arms in the bullpen,
preventing having to use high-leverage relievers if the
game wasn't in the balance.

The Brewers also had the scheduling quirk of no
games scheduled on any Thursday during the month.
The Cubs were playing an onerous schedule in
September, including rain makeups, but the Brewers
played a heavy slate earlier and now were enjoying the
benefits of the same day off every week. Certain starters
would get extra rest. Others could have turns skipped.

Counsell had two hot pitchers – veterans Jhoulys
Chacín and Wade Miley – who were doing stellar work
nearly every time out. Junior Guerra had pitched
himself out of the rotation with a horrible August,
and Chase Anderson and Zach Davies seemed best
served with shorter stints. Gio Gonzalez, acquired for

the final month, had suffered through a tough season with Washington, prompting Counsell to keep him on a somewhat short leash, with tremendous results.

Analytics had taken over how games were being run, leading some to say baseball was being managed by the numbers. Those numbers showed lineups had more trouble facing relievers from the sixth inning on than getting more looks at the starters. That approach was reinforced if your bullpen was dominant, and the Brewers certainly fit that mold.

It was a methodology commonly referred to as "bullpening," and the Brewers could not be accused of lagging behind. Over the final month of the season, Milwaukee would play 26 games, and only twice would a starting pitcher go as many as six innings, and never more.

Gone were the days that 100 pitches were the goal for starters to reach, usually signaling the end of their night. Counsell regularly pulled pitchers while in the 70s and 80s, often while they were still performing effectively. Pitch counts no longer were the overriding factor in making changes, as they had been in the past.

Long before reaching that final month, Counsell discouraged members of the media covering the team from using the terms "starters" and "relievers." He considered every game a group effort of the entire staff, merely calling his pitchers "out-getters." It was all about getting 27 outs, Counsell explained, no matter how many pitchers it took to do so.

Each night, Counsell and Johnson would plan out the best route to get those 27 outs, taking into account bullpen availability and pitcher/hitter matchups, among other factors. Adjustments would have to be made in some games, of course. You can only script nine innings to a certain point, given the unpredictability of baseball, including random luck.

In a three-game sweep of San Francisco at Miller Park at the end of the first home stand of the month, Anderson went five innings, Gonzalez covered 5 2/3 innings and Davies turned in another five-inning stint. That left the bullpen to cover 11 1/3 innings, which the relief corps did without problems.

In the finale of that series, the Brewers faced Giants ace Madison Bumgarner, whose season was marred by a broken hand suffered when hit by a liner off the bat of Kansas City's Whit Merrifield during exhibition play. Bumgarner never got back on track fully after returning to action but on this Sunday afternoon was throwing the ball well, taking a 2-1 lead into the bottom of the sixth.

The crafty lefty had retired 15 hitters in a row when Christian Yelich kept the inning alive with a two-out walk. Jesús Aguilar followed with an opposite-field single to right, bringing up Ryan Braun, who had driven in the Brewers' only run with a first-inning double.

It was at that point that Bumgarner got himself in trouble with a bit of gamesmanship. His first pitch to Braun was up and in, forcing him to bail out of the batter's box so fast his momentum carried him up the third-base line a few steps. Two pitches later, Bumgarner came inside again, plunking Braun.

Bumgarner didn't just lose his control suddenly but nobody was sure what Braun had done to piss him off. The pitcher, of course, played innocent after the game, leaving Braun to speculate what raised his hackles.

"I had a real long at-bat, my second at-bat, flew out, took a pretty good swing," Braun recalled. "I jogged by him and I think maybe he thought I said something that I didn't say. I told him, 'Good pitch, good battle.' Something like that, and maybe he misunderstood me. I don't know."

Whatever the issue, Braun didn't like having pitches come near his head while staring into the glare of the afternoon sun. He walked slowly toward first, glaring at Bumgarner, catcher Nick Hundley acting as escort, but the Brewers' dugout began to empty, as did the Giants' dugout, resulting in mostly chatter.

The conflict took a different turn when home plate umpire Tom Hallion issued warnings to both benches against any retaliation. Since his pitchers hadn't done anything wrong, Counsell took exception to that decision and came out to let Hallion know about. Before you knew it, the two were face to face, screaming at each other, veins bulging in Counsell's neck. Hallion finally had enough and ejected Counsell, who got in some parting shots before departing. When the woofing continued from the Brewers' dugout, Hallion decided to give Counsell some company, tossing Miley and rookie catcher Jacob Nottingham.

With order finally restored, second baseman Jonathan Schoop stepped into the box with the bases loaded, looking for something to go right for a change. Seeking to add more pop to his lineup before the July 31 trade deadline, general manager David Stearns acquired third baseman Mike Moustakas from Kansas City, then traded with Baltimore for Schoop to provide a right-handed alternative with pop.

But Schoop never got going at the plate. He staggered to a terrible start, playing four games before collecting a hit, and began pressing to show the trade was not a mistake, only digging the hole deeper. In 32 games with his new team, the native of Curacao was batting a mere .216 with three home runs and 13 RBI, prompting Counsell to reduce his playing time.

That trend continued against Bumgarner as Schoop struck out in his first two at-bats. Bumgarner, perhaps unnerved by the silliness he had started, fell behind in the count, 2-1, before throwing a cutter that he tried to get in on Schoop's hands. He didn't get the pitch in far enough and Schoop yanked it down the left-field line for a grand slam, turning the 2-1 deficit into a 5-2 lead.

As Schoop floated around the bases exuberantly, pandemonium became the order of the day, both in the Miller Park stands and the Brewers' dugout. Players leaped onto the field to greet him after he crossed the plate, a raucous celebration that breached major-league baseball etiquette, prompting first base umpire Dan Bellino to shoo them back into the dugout.

"It was like the winter league, the WBC (World Baseball Classic), kind of," Schoop said. "You hit a home run, everybody comes out. It was really fun."

Bumgarner had allowed the Brewers up for air by throwing at Braun, and they made him pay. In what was otherwise a terrible two months with Milwaukee, Schoop finally managed to deliver a defining moment, and it was a big one.

"It was a moment I'll never forget," said Schoop, finally able to flash a big smile and exhale a bit.

The sweep concluded a 6-1 home stand, drawing the Brewers within two games of Chicago as they headed for Wrigley Field and yet another showdown with the Cubs.

This race was starting to get very interesting.

In the first two series of the season between the teams, Chicago's pitching staff dominated the Brewers, tossing five shutouts in eight games. But the pendulum had begun to swing in the other direction, with the Cubs' offense scuffling in the final weeks and Milwaukee's staff taking advantage.

Miley took the mound in the opener, which again was a good thing for the Brewers. The Cubs countered with veteran lefty Jon Lester, pitching on two days rest because his previous outing was rained out after one inning in Washington. With the score tied, 2-2, in the sixth, Lester retired the first two hitters before surrendering a single by Moustakas and double by Erik Kratz.

At that point, Lester began experiencing back spasms that forced him from the game, which immediately worked to the Brewers' benefit. Carl Edwards Jr., whose control issues were a factor in the Labor Day loss in Milwaukee, skipped his first pitch past catcher Willson Contreras for a run-scoring wild pitch that put Milwaukee up to stay.

As Edwards prepared to throw that pitch, Brewers third base coach Ed Sedar leaned over and whispered to Moustakas to be ready to go on a wild pitch, almost as if he had a premonition.

"And it happened," said Moustakas, who took a big secondary lead off the bag. "I was able to get down there. It worked out pretty well for us."

Sticking with quick-hook method of handling his "initial out-getters," Counsell pulled Miley after five innings and only 81 pitches. Rookie Corbin Burnes, who worked his way into the manager's confidence by excelling time after time in tough spots, pitched a scoreless sixth before turning it over to the fearless Hader, who completely overpowered the Cubs, striking out all six hitters he faced.

Jeffress closed out Chicago with little difficulty in the ninth, and just like that, the Brewers were a game out of first place. It would have been cause for greater concern for the Cubs if not for the fact they had the great equalizer on the mound the next day, Brewers killer José Quintana. That almost always guaranteed a Cubs victory, and this would be no exception.

With Quintana shutting out the Brewers on three hits over 6 2/3 innings, Chicago squeezed out a 3-0 victory, their sixth shutout victory of the season over Milwaukee. Chacín lost a match-up with Quintana for the second consecutive meeting but didn't deserve being saddled with an "L," allowing just one hit over five innings.

Chicago manager Joe Maddon knew a good thing when he saw it, and made sure Quintana was lined up to face the Brewers in all six series during the season, no easy feat of scheduling. Quintana went 4-1 with a 2.17 ERA in those meetings, with the Cubs taking five of the six games.

The Brewers and Cubs would meet for the last time the next evening – or so they thought – with a win nearly a must for Milwaukee to stay in the division race. A loss would put the Brewers three behind the Cubs with 15 to play, a daunting challenge.

"We're running out of time," acknowledged Travis Shaw. "Three games back with 15 left is not ideal. We need to win the series. We came in here knowing we had to win the series to have a shot at the division."

With so much at stake, Counsell had a shorter leash than usual on his "initial out-getter." With the pitcher's spot due up first in the top of the fifth, he pulled Anderson, who was throwing a two-hit shutout on only 71 pitches. Counsell would call on five relievers to cover the final 15 outs but as usual, the key outings were turned in by his three rock stars, Knebel, Hader and Jeffress, who combined to blank Chicago over 3 2/3 innings, with six strikeouts.

The Brewers were clinging to a 2-1 lead in the ninth when Curtis Granderson ignited a three-run rally with a home run off reliever Steve Cishek. This was why general manager David Stearns pulled off a trade late on August 31 with Toronto to acquire the 37-year-old veteran, whose postseason experience, veteran leadership and gas remaining in his tank paid off in a big way on this night.

The 5-1 victory pulled the Brewers back within a game of the Cubs, who couldn't help feeling their hard-charging rivals breathing down their necks. After winning seven of the first eight meetings between the teams, Chicago dropped seven of the next 10, getting out-pitched much of the time by the Brewers' unheralded staff.

It was Milwaukee's seventh consecutive series victory and their 11th win in 14 games. It was obvious to everyone, in particular, Chicago's North Siders, that the Brewers weren't going away. In a span of only 10 days, they had gone from five games behind the Cubs to only one. They still had the safety net of leading the Wild Card race but no one in the visiting clubhouse that day was focused on that consolation prize.

"We've still got a ways to go," said Lorenzo Cain, who sliced and diced Chicago's pitchers for eight hits in 14 at-bats in the series while also making two highlight-reel catches in center field. "Nothing is finished yet. We've got some tough matchups coming. We've got to definitely bring our 'A' game."

With six of their next nine games against Pittsburgh, the Brewers would have to figure out a way to beat the mediocre Pirates. They were 4-9 against them for the season, and couldn't afford many more stumbles.

CHAPTER EIGHTEEN

Born to manage the Brewers

Craig Counsell was born to manage the Brewers. If that sounds a bit far-fetched, know that his path in life was destined to lead him back at some point to the club, where his father, John, worked in the front office in the 1980s.

Young Craig tagged along with his dad to County Stadium whenever he could, hanging out at times with the players. A photo of pre-teen Craig, holding one of his baseball trophies and sitting between Hall of Fame reliever Rollie Fingers and outfielder Dion James, is a prized family possession that likely created jealousy among friends at the time.

Craig grew up in Whitefish Bay, a cozy village north of Milwaukee, and played baseball at the local high school. Colleges weren't fighting over his services, but John Counsell wanted his son to follow in his footsteps at Notre Dame if at all possible. So, the proud dad reached out to new Fighting Irish coach Pat Murphy in a bit of reverse recruiting in 1988, pitching his son's talents and baseball IQ.

Murphy was invited to an informal workout at County Stadium that included Sal Bando Jr., son of the Brewers' general manager at the time. The young Bando instead would attend Arizona State, where Murphy later would coach. But Craig showed enough for Murphy to invite him to Notre Dame, where his baseball skills were honed over four formative years that included earning a degree in accounting.

Counsell was selected in the 11th round of the 1992 draft by the Colorado Rockies, who wouldn't keep him long. But Counsell would go on to a 15-year career in the majors, making himself valuable by showing he

Brewers manager Craig Counsell shares a laugh with Mr. Baseball—
Brewers legendary announcer, Bob Uecker.
AP PHOTO

could play all over the infield, understanding defensive versatility was coveted.

Counsell had a knack for being in the right place at the right time, playing for World Series champions in Florida in 1997 and Arizona in 2001. He scored the winning run for the Marlins in the 11th inning of Game 7 against Cleveland, and participated in the winning ninth-inning rally for the Diamondbacks in Game 7 against the vaunted Yankees. Forrest Gump would have been proud.

After the 2003 season, Brewers general manager Doug Melvin traded slugger Richie Sexson to Arizona for a package of six players, looking to restock an empty pantry. One of those players acquired was Counsell, who became the Brewers starting shortstop in 2004. He would return to the Diamondbacks for a couple of seasons before coming home for good to Milwaukee, where he played his last five seasons.

Counsell helped the Brewers end a 26-year playoff drought by claiming the National League Wild Card berth in 2008, and played on an even better team in 2011 that advanced to the NLCS before getting knocked off by eventual World Series champion St. Louis. He retired after that season and was offered a job as an advisor to Melvin, a role he used to learn the front-office side of the game.

It was assumed at the time that Counsell's future in baseball would be as a general manager, but he never felt pigeon-holed in that regard, nor did his father feel that way.

"Some people saw him only as a GM because he was supposedly in training for it," John Counsell said. "But he could do a lot of things. I think he could be president of the Brewers if he wanted."

In 2014, Counsell was included on the candidate list for the managerial opening in Tampa Bay but later removed himself from consideration. He did not want to uproot wife Michelle and their four children from their life in Whitefish Bay or spend that much time away from them should he get the job.

Counsell didn't need to mull his next managerial offer. One month into the 2015 season, he replaced Brewers manager Ron Roenicke, reluctantly fired by Melvin after the team staggered to a 7-18 start. Given the opportunity to manage his hometown team, Counsell never considered declining.

Melvin knew Counsell was the right man for the job after interacting with him in the front office for more than three years. The two would sit in Melvin's office, discussing the game, what other teams were doing, analyzing players on the Brewers' roster as well as those on the other side of the field.

It became evident to Melvin that Counsell was a true student of the game, was well-connected in the industry and well-respected. He was known as a great teammate when he played, and Melvin was certain he'd encourage his players to be great teammates as well. All things considered, it seemed like the perfect fit.

"He knew how the game was going to be changing," Melvin said. "That was important. He knew the game was going to more of an analytical mode and looking for new ways to do things. He was on board with that. That transition from the front office to the manager's seat was much easier."

Counsell understood the Brewers were about to undergo a large-scale rebuilding process, virtually guaranteeing many losing seasons. Not exactly the greatest situation for a new manager looking to establish himself in the majors but he was the perfect choice in terms of temperament, experience and pedigree. Process would take precedence over results, at least for a period of time.

At his introductory press conference, an emotional Counsell made it clear just how much it meant to manage the Brewers.

"I'm a Milwaukee Brewer," he said. "I've always felt that way. Baseball in this city is important to me. It's part of me. I feel a responsibility for it. I always have.

"It's not surreal. It's a place where I feel like I've prepared myself to be. It's an honor and it's humbling but I feel like this is what I was meant to do."

Later, it was announced that Melvin would step aside and a search for a new GM would begin as part of the team overhaul. The choice to replace him was David Stearns, the assistant GM at Houston and at age 30, some 14 years younger than Counsell.

Quite often when new general managers come in, they seek a hand-picked manager, sooner or later. But principal owner Mark Attanasio and his search committee made it clear to each candidate that he would be expected to work with Counsell, who had been given a three-year contract. Stearns had no issue with that caveat, paving the way for a partnership that would become hugely successful.

"It would have disqualified a candidate if he had a problem with that," Attanasio said.

As expected, the Brewers took their lumps in 2015, losing 94 games. There was slight improvement the next season, when Counsell nurtured budding major leaguers who would become keepers to a 73-89 record. Players were coming and going at a furious pace but Counsell kept his team focused on the goal of constant improvement, even if it came in small increments.

The big breakthrough occurred in 2017, when the team morphed from the rebuilding Brewers to the contending Brewers. Counsell was given a three-year extension before that season, a huge vote of confidence from Stearns that demonstrated they were in this together, with no separate agendas.

Milwaukee stayed in the hunt for the second Wild Card berth until the penultimate day of the season, finishing with an 87-76 record, an increase of 14 victories from the previous season. With Stearns pulling the personnel strings and Counsell banding the players together with his "stay connected" mantra, success on the field came sooner than expected. Much sooner.

Though Counsell played his career before analytics became a driving force in how the game is played, he quickly adapted to new-era baseball. He sifted through reams of information, decided what was and wasn't pertinent to winning, and began using numbers to his benefit, and to his team's benefit. Stearns put together a growing analytics department that broke down the game in every facet, and Counsell willingly joined the revolution.

Attanasio recalled bumping into Counsell in the spring of 2016, when the Brewers were just beginning to dive head-first into the deep end of the analytics pool. A consulting group was brought in that did advance video scouting instead of using actual, human scouts, and the first person to enter the room was the Milwaukee manager.

"He stayed for like 2½ hours, so I knew he was open to new ideas," Attanasio recalled. "This is a man who (was part of winning rallies) in two World Series. He felt like all he had to do in baseball, which was a big task, was to win a World Series for the Milwaukee Brewers. That meant a lot to me."

Managing a baseball team is more than crunching numbers, however. Otherwise, your tax accountant could handle the double switches. A manager has to know how to lead players, motivate them, communicate with them, coddle them, kick them in the butt, and most important, put them in the best situations in which they can succeed.

As it turned out, Counsell excelled in each of those areas. His leadership skills were evident from the outset, keeping his team focused during the tough early days of the rebuild and showing patience when the players needed time to figure out the big leagues. He continued to preach having each other's backs, realizing the importance of sticking together when things looked bleak.

Counsell was adept at problem solving, so he didn't worry when the acquisitions of Lorenzo Cain and Christian Yelich gave him more outfielders than places to play them. He believed firmly in using every player on the team to achieve success, to the point where he refused to designate starting players and bench players. Instead, he referred to all non-pitchers as his position player group.

The challenge of finding playing time for everyone became greater in July and August, when a series of trades injected new blood into the mix. That task became even tougher in September, when expanded rosters provided more players than you could count. Counsell continued to emphasize the all-for-one approach to the game and his players bought into it, in large part because they trusted their manager.

"He has demonstrated during his time managing here that he's very skilled at putting major-league players in positions to succeed," said Stearns. "It's one of the keys to being a good major-league manager – recognizing the strengths of your players. At the end of the day, that's all you can do."

As with every manager, Counsell heard his share of criticism, mostly for bullpen management. No facet of managing creates firestorms quite like pitching changes, the most difficult part of running a game. If you leave the starter in too long and he gets tattooed, you are barbequed for not going to your bullpen. If you yank the starter and the first reliever coughs up the lead, you were an idiot for making the change.

But Counsell knew where his managerial bread was buttered, and it was with liberal use of a killer bullpen. As for the stress of the job, he usually shrugged that off with a smile and positive comment.

"I'm having fun, man," Counsell said when asked about leading his team through the darkness of rebuilding and into the light of contending baseball. "It's a responsibility. You want to make something special happen for the baseball fans in Wisconsin. If I can play a part in doing that, it makes me happy."

Counsell was born to manage the Brewers, and the majority of the team's fans couldn't be happier to have one of their own in charge.

CHAPTER NINETEEN

Flipping the script on the Cards

Why couldn't the Brewers beat the Pirates?

It was a question manager Craig Counsell was hearing more and more, and he had no answers. That's because there were none. The Brewers were leading the Wild Card race and breathing down the necks of the NL Central-leading Cubs. The Pirates were fighting to stay above .500, languishing in fourth place in the division, another season slipping away.

In particular, the Brewers had trouble scoring runs against the Pirates, who despite treading water as a team had a solid pitching staff, led by burgeoning ace Trevor Williams. The Pirates thought they were bolstering their rotation even more by trading for Tampa Bay's Chris Archer, but he was having trouble gaining traction.

In the opener of a three-game series at Miller Park on September 14, the Brewers jumped on Archer for three runs in the first inning, with Christian Yelich and Travis Shaw taking him deep. The stage was set for a rare offensive outbreak against the Pirates, resulting in a 7-4 victory, the Brewers' 12th in their last 14 games.

The Brewers hoped the worm finally had turned but it was back to the deep freeze for their offense in the next two games. In the process, their chances of catching the Cubs took a hit. Big right-hander Ivan Nova had his way with the Brewers in the second game, holding them to four hits and one run over six innings as Pittsburgh held on for a 3-1 victory. After Yelich's first-inning home run against Nova, it was a whole lot of nothing for the rest of the game.

Pittsburgh's pitching staff was more formidable than most folks realized but this was getting beyond frustrating for the Brewers. The loss left them 5-10 against the Pirates for the season, and in the 10 losses they had scored a grand total of 21 runs. You're not going to win many games averaging a mere 2.1 runs.

Every season, one team seems to have the number of another team, even the good ones, and for Milwaukee it was Pittsburgh. The inexplicable domination by an otherwise average team was putting a huge crimp in the Brewers' hopes of winning the division. They now were 2½ games behind Chicago, three in the loss column, with 13 games to play. The math was becoming problematic, any way you looked at it.

In even worse news, the Pirates saved their best pitcher, Williams, for last in the series. He was quietly putting together one of the best seasons among NL starters, and the Brewers knew they had their work cut out to extend their streak of seven consecutive winning series.

The Brewers' worst fears were realized when Williams showed up in the finale with his good stuff, blanking them on two hits over six innings. Jhoulys Chacín, who had taken consecutive tough-luck losses with little run support, would suffer that fate again, falling to 14-8 despite allowing only three hits and two runs in five innings.

Milwaukee's offensive drought reached 16 consecutive scoreless innings until Jesús Aguilar and Domingo Santana homered on consecutive pitches in the ninth off Pirates flame-throwing closer Felipe Vázquez. But it wasn't enough to avoid a 3-2 loss, leaving the Brewers 5-11 against Pittsburgh for the season.

It was the first time the Brewers dropped consecutive games since mid-August. The good news was that the Cubs lost to the Reds, leaving them 2½ games ahead of Milwaukee. The bad news was that the Brewers had three more games coming up against the Pirates at PNC Park, where they were 1-6 for the season.

First would come three games at home against the Reds, whom the Brewers continued to dominate, taking two of three to run their record to 13-6 against Cincinnati for the season. The Reds were just as tired of losing to Milwaukee as the Brewers were of losing to

Pittsburgh. Such is baseball. Trying to figure out such things only made your head hurt.

One thing was certain: The Brewers could not afford another losing series against the Pirates as they headed for Pittsburgh and their last road trip of the season. They were 2½ games behind the Cubs with 10 to play. Time was running out if they wanted to avoid the one-game crap shoot known as the Wild Card Game.

As it turned out, the Brewers needed Mother Nature to intercede to finally experience something positive against the Pirates' pitching staff. Nova, who chewed through Milwaukee's batting order six days earlier at Miller Park, was doing so again in the series opener when a rainstorm inundated PNC Park and stopped play for 2 hours and 14 minutes. Nova's night came to a premature end and the Brewers went to work against the Pirates' bullpen when play resumed.

Shaw, Moustakas and Erik Kratz homered during a six-run outburst in the sixth and the Brewers pulled away to an 8-3 victory, scoring more runs than in any game in Pittsburgh since September 4, 2016. The rare romp pulled them within 1½ games of Chicago while maintaining a three-game lead over St. Louis for the first Wild Card spot, which guaranteed home-field advantage in that game.

What would have happened had the rains not come and Nova continued pitching? The Brewers didn't know, and they didn't care.

"I just think having a good night here, period (is big)," said Counsell, who had another masterful game of manipulating his bullpen after Chacín saw his start end prematurely upon yielding to a pinch-hitter in the fifth. Counsell used his five best relief arms – Corbin Burnes, Josh Hader, Corey Knebel, Joakim Soria and Jeremy Jeffress – to throttle the Pirates' attack on three hits over five scoreless innings, never letting them up for air.

Hader was in the midst of another of his head-shaking strikeout binges, running his string of consecutive punchouts to 16 before Corey Dickerson tripled with two down in the sixth. Knebel, who put behind him the command issues that plagued him earlier in the season, struck out both hitters he faced and was en route to NL Reliever of the Month for September.

Counsell and pitching coach Derek Johnson continued to look ahead at the schedule and ponder every possible advantage they could muster from it. Accordingly, they tweaked the rotation and moved Chacín up a day to line him up for the potential Wild Card shootout. As it turned out, he would pitch in a much different and even more important contest to finish the season.

The euphoria over the offense's long-overdue breakthrough quickly subsided when the Brewers once again faced Williams, the hottest pitcher in the league, the next night. The result was predictable as he blanked them on four harmless singles over six innings, allowing Pittsburgh to make off with a 3-0 victory.

The Brewers had faced Williams three times and lost to him each time, failing to score even one run over 19 innings. That is what you call total domination. The combination of Williams' deceptive delivery and the pinpoint command he had demonstrated for many weeks proved too much for Milwaukee's hitters, who were shut out for the 12th time.

On the topic of domination, the Pirates boosted their record to 12-6 against Milwaukee for the season, including a 7-2 mark at PNC Park. Imagine the difference in the standings had the Brewers merely broken even in those 18 games against the fourth-place team in the division. As it was, the loss dropped them 2 ½ games behind the Cubs with seven to play and trimmed their Wild Card lead to two games over the Cardinals.

"It seems like every year there's a team like that for every team, and it's Pittsburgh for us this year," Shaw said. "It kind of sucks. Bad timing."

Unable to afford another defeat before a huge three-game series in St. Louis, the Brewers rose to the occasion in what became a cathartic experience. Busting loose for five runs in the second and five more in the sixth, they cruised to a 13-6 rout behind home runs from Yelich, Shaw and Moustakas, thoroughly enjoying the oh-so-rare laugher against the Pirates.

It was Milwaukee's biggest offensive outburst in Pittsburgh since obliterating the Pirates, 20-0, on April 22, 2010. Where had this attack been all season against Pittsburgh's underrated pitching staff? A relieved Counsell really didn't care when asked that question.

"We won the game, and that's all that matters," said Counsell, who again went to his bullpen early and often upon pulling starter Wade Miley after four innings. "We won the series and put ourselves in a good spot."

A good spot, indeed. Beyond remaining 2½ games behind the Cubs, the Brewers reduced their magic number for clinching a Wild Card berth to four games. They were that close to their first postseason appearance in seven years, and they could taste it.

Afterward, Counsell showed he had more pitching tricks up his sleeve. He scratched his scheduled starter for the series opener in St. Louis, Chase Anderson, announcing he would go with a bullpen day in the crucial game. Anderson had been a regular in the rotation since coming to the Brewers before the 2016 season but hadn't been himself for some time, struggling with his release point and making too many mistakes over the plate, leading to an alarming number of 30 home runs, most in the league.

Anderson had faltered too often in the first inning of his starts, compiling a 6.30 ERA over 30 outings. He had been kept on a tight leash throughout the final month, never going more than five innings. Counsell did not reveal which reliever would start the next day at Busch Stadium, saying the decision would be made on the charter flight from Pittsburgh.

The bullpen had been the strength of the club all season, and Counsell had plenty of arms to choose from with expanded September rosters. That mix included three former starters, Junior Guerra, Freddy Peralta and Brandon Woodruff. Still, it took guts for Counsell to make the call with so much at stake, knowing full well that Anderson's ego would be wounded.

"Obviously, it's frustrating," said Anderson, who had a 2.65 ERA in six career starts in St. Louis. "I want to pitch every time that my name is called. I want to be the guy on the mound regardless of what the situation is but sometimes you've got to swallow your pride."

Counsell couldn't worry about hurt feelings at this critical stage of the season. He was known, for good reason, as a players' manager, one who kept lines of communication open and never bad-mouthed one of his troops in public. But this was the time to put team ahead of player and pull out all the stops, and that's exactly what he was going to do.

As it turned out, Counsell didn't plan to go with a bullpen day in the normal sense of that term. What he had in mind all along was an "opener," a tactic that was becoming used more throughout the majors, with the biggest trend-setter being the Tampa Bay Rays. That strategy meant using a relief pitcher at the outset to match up against certain lineups before inserting a starting type into the game. Anything to throw an opponents' game plan off at the outset and give your team an edge.

Counsell's "opener" would not stick around for long, however. Left-handed reliever Dan Jennings was used solely to retire Cardinals leadoff hitter Matt Carpenter, a lefty swinger who had been devouring right-handed pitching while soaring near the top of the league's home run leader board. After Jennings retired Carpenter on a grounder to second, he exited in favor of rookie righty Freddy Peralta, who took regular turns in the rotation earlier in the season.

Jennings threw only three pitches, leading to one of the funniest quotes of the season after the game.

"Somebody asked me before the game if I was going to go five tonight," he revealed. "I said, 'Five pitches or five innings?'"

Counsell merely wanted to reduce the number of at-bats by Carpenter against Peralta, and it became evident why in third inning when the dangerous hitter doubled in a run to tie the score, 1-1. As it turned out, that was the only run Peralta yielded in a solid 3 2/3 innings. After the game, Counsell would say, "Freddy did exactly what we wanted. He got 11 outs."

The Brewers had more to worry about than Carpenter's at-bats. To emerge with a huge 6-4 victory, they had to overcome a rare blowup inning by Hader as well as a rain delay that came too late to save him.

With a 3-1 lead in the sixth, Counsell summoned Hader, as he had done so successfully at that stage of games throughout the season. But, in a span of three batters, the 3-1 lead turned into a 4-3 deficit, stunning Hader and his teammates. José Martínez led off with a home run to center, Paul DeJong drew a walk and Marcell Ozuna sent a drive out to left-center for a two-run shot.

It was raining as Hader faced those batters, and the Busch Stadium radar gun showed his velocity was down a few clicks. Hader, who had struck out 20 of the last 25 hitters he faced entering the game and had not allowed a homer since Chicago's Anthony Rizzo got him on Labor Day, was asked afterward if he had trouble gripping the ball. In typical humble fashion, he refused to use that as an excuse.

Making the outing scarier, Hader slipped and fell, spinning to make a pickoff move to second base. He could have easily strained a groin or hamstring but escaped injury, only to see the umpires finally halt play the next inning, result in a 31-minute delay.

The Brewers drew even on a run-scoring groundout by Yelich in the seventh, then accepted a gift run in the eighth when the Cardinals botched a pickoff play at first base. The torrid Yelich doubled in another run in the ninth, providing a two-run cushion that Knebel had no problems protecting, striking out the side to end it.

For some time, a running joke between Counsell and reporters covering the team was that every game was "the biggest game of the year," but this one actually fit that bill. The Brewers' magic number for clinching a playoff berth dropped to three games, and with the Cubs losing to the Pirates, 5-1, the division lead narrowed to 1½ games.

As for possibly catching the Cubs, Ryan Braun said, "I think it's a benefit for us to feel like we're chasing them instead of just having teams chase us. Until you're mathematically eliminated, of course it's a possibility."

Earlier that day, as players reported to the ballpark to prepare for the huge series, Braun strutted into the visiting clubhouse and proclaimed to teammates that he was ready to "dominate the rest of the way." Braun never lacked for confidence, so it wasn't totally out of character, but the point he was trying to make was that the various maladies that plagued him periodically throughout the season had subsided, leaving him feeling energized. As the Cardinals would discover during the series, it was not an idle boast.

As he got closer to the end of his career, and with the team in rebuilding mode, Braun wasn't sure he'd see October baseball again in a Milwaukee uniform, and was determined to do everything in his power to make it happen. That was quite evident the next night when Braun slammed two home runs and Yelich continued his blistering MVP pursuit with six RBI, leading the way to a 12-4 laugher.

The victory reduced the magic number for clinching a playoff spot to one, but the players had a bigger target in sight. With the Cubs losing again at home to pesky Pittsburgh, their division lead was a mere half-game over hard-charging Milwaukee. What seemed unattainable not that long ago now seemed completely doable, and nobody was giving up hope.

All the Brewers had to do to clinch their first playoff berth in seven years was complete a three-game sweep over the Cardinals the next night. The Cubs announced they wouldn't hold a celebration merely for making the playoffs, preferring to wait for a third consecutive NL Central crown. But the Brewers had no intention of waiting to party, not after shocking the baseball world by becoming competitive again far ahead of schedule.

Another factor in planning a celebration was the many indignities St. Louis had inflicted on the Brewers over the years, beginning in 1982 when they won the final two games to claim the World Series. It took nearly 30 years for Milwaukee to return to that level again, only again to be stymied in the 2011 NLCS by the Cardinals, who went on to another world championship.

The Brewers wanted nothing more than to party in the Busch Stadium visiting clubhouse and let the Cardinals feel the figurative sting of champagne spraying on the other side. It was with that motivation that travel director Dan Larrea, clubhouse director Tony Migliaccio and equipment manager Jason Shawger made sure there was plenty of bubbly on hand as the Brewers took the field for the series finale.

To be sure, Larrea rented a truck in Milwaukee, loaded it with champagne, and had it driven to Pittsburgh at the start of the trip, in the event a playoff berth was clinched there. The truck then was driven to St. Louis, with the possibility of returning home to Miller Park if nothing special happened at Busch Stadium.

Counsell had the pitcher he wanted on the mound, Chacín, who had lost three consecutive starts but pitched well in each one, the victim of scant run support. The Cardinals, desperate to remain in the Wild Card race, went with unheralded rookie John Gant, who showed up with his good stuff.

Counsell remarked at the outset of the series that he hadn't seen a player as hot as Yelich since Barry Bonds terrorized NL pitchers en route to the all-time home run crown. And, right on cue, St. Louis gave Yelich the Bonds treatment, walking him in each of his five trips to the plate.

Shaw made the Cardinals pay by knocking in Yelich twice and Chacín made those runs stand up, allowing only one hit and one run through five innings. Following his now-familiar pattern of bullpen usage, Counsell removed him at that point, giving his bullpen four innings to cover to clinch the playoffs.

Sometimes, the baseball gods smile on an upstart team about to do something big, and that was the case in the eighth inning as St. Louis tried to mount a tying rally against Hader. The gritty Carpenter overcame the usual lefty vs. lefty disadvantage by drawing a two-out walk, keeping the inning alive for Martínez. Well aware that Martínez had taken Hader deep in that series opener, Counsell did not hesitate to summon Jeffress.

Jeffress jammed Martínez, getting him to hit a tapper to third baseman Mike Moustakas, who charged in and fired past first base for an error. This was where the baseball gods stepped in. Adolis Garcia, a speedster inserted to run for Carpenter, came flying around the bases and surely was going to score the tying run, only to stumble rounding third and tumble to the ground.

That pratfall allowed second baseman Hernán Pérez to chase down the ball in foul territory, near the rolled-up tarp, and throw to Kratz, who wheeled to try a phantom tag, only to discover Garcia had fallen and was nowhere near the plate. The mortified runner surrendered unconditionally, and the Brewers' 2-1 lead was safe.

The game ended with Jeffress striking out pinch-hitter Tyler O'Neill, then letting out a mighty roar on the mound before being mobbed by his teammates. Braun, the only active player who was part of Milwaukee's last playoff team in 2011, tried to put it all in perspective as the party raged on in the visiting clubhouse.

"What we accomplished is not something you see with other organizations," said Braun, removing the goggles used to shield his eyes from the champagne spray. "We never really had a significant period which most teams do when they go through a significant rebuild and retooling phase. I just hope this is the first celebration and not the last."

In Chicago, the Cubs had pulled out a 7-6 victory in 10 innings over the Pirates, keeping them a half-game ahead. The next day, while the Brewers were off, the Cubs would win again to go up by one game with three to play. Milwaukee would return home for an interleague series against woeful Detroit. Chicago stayed home to play the Cardinals, guaranteed to be a spirited battle between two teams that didn't like each other.

The off day couldn't have been better timed for the Brewers. It allowed them to party a little later in St. Louis, continue the fun on the flight home and then sleep late in the morning, no doubt with sweet dreams.

"Everyone should get to enjoy this, embrace it," said the widely beaming Braun. "This is an incredible accomplishment, and everyone has contributed to it."

The Brewers were guaranteed a home Wild Card game, at the very least, but they had bigger plans. They had come this far. Why stop now?

CHAPTER TWENTY

162 games aren't enough

Somebody forgot to tell the lowly Detroit Tigers that their final series of the season, an oddly timed interleague trip to Milwaukee, was meaningless. With 95 losses entering the weekend, they should have been marking time, planning fishing and hunting trips.

It was the Brewers who had everything to win, and therefore everything to lose, as they returned home to Miller Park one game behind the Cubs in the NL Central, still eyeing home-field advantage throughout the postseason and avoidance of a possible one-and-done in the Wild Card Game.

The Tigers showed immediately they came to play, scoring three runs in the top of the first off Zach Davies, who suffered a series of paper-cut hits, bleeders that found holes and went through. The sellout crowd of 44,770 got more than a bit nervous watching that agonizing rally, but the Brewers answered with three runs in the bottom of the inning, with Christian Yelich continuing his unconscious hitting binge with a two-run homer and reinvigorated Ryan Braun also knocking one out.

Davies settled down after the first but got the usual September early-hook from Counsell, exiting after four innings to make it yet another bullpen game. But Counsell's decision to bat for Davies in the bottom of the fourth paid off handsomely, with Domingo Santana delivering a run-scoring single to give the Brewers a 5-3 lead.

One of four prospects acquired from Houston in the July 2015 trade that sent center fielder Carlos Gomez and pitcher Mike Fiers to the Astros, Santana was a key figure in the club's leap forward in '17, smashing 30 home runs with 85 RBI as the everyday right fielder. But something mysterious happened to him at the outset of the 2018 season, robbing him of the power that made him special.

Santana appeared to be an odd man out after the January acquisitions of outfielders Lorenzo Cain and Yelich but Counsell found him enough playing time to do some damage. Instead, Santana played his way onto the bench and eventually to the minors in June, a puzzling turn of events.

"It's not something you want to do," Counsell said on the day Santana was optioned to Class AAA Colorado Springs with a .249 batting average and only three home runs. "He was a big part of our success last year. We just need to get him going. Hopefully, he can get it going down there."

But Santana continued to falter at Colorado Springs, considered a hitter's haven. He would remain there until being recalled in September as rosters were allowed to expand. It was too late to recover an everyday role but Counsell began using him as a bat off the bench, and to Santana's credit, he put the year's disappointment behind him and delivered one big hit after another.

The Tigers didn't roll over, however. They tied the game in the eighth off reliever Josh Hader, whose recent slide continued when he surrendered a two-run homer to Dawel Lugo, a .209 hitter. Hader, who had no trouble keeping the ball in the park all season, now had surrendered three home runs over three outings, showing some wear and tear after a long season of mostly overpowering, multi-inning outings.

It was the first homer in the majors for Lugo, and it sucked the air out of the packed house. But, much like the blade of grass that tripped pinch-runner Adolis Garcia rounding third in St. Louis two days earlier, wiping out the potential tying run, the Brewers were about to catch another hard-to-believe break.

Leading off the bottom of the inning, Braun reached out on a 2-2 slider from Tigers reliever Victor Alcántara and sent it deep to right field. The ball carried to the wall, where Nicholas Castellanos made a leap and got a glove on it. Castellanos wasn't able to squeeze it, however, and the ball popped out and rolled for a bit on the top of the padding before softly dropping over to the other side for Braun's second homer of the game and the decisive run in Milwaukee's 6-5 squeaker.

"I couldn't tell if it would have been a homer or not (without Castellanos' help)," Braun said. "I think it might have gone off the top of the wall. Who knows what would have happened from there?"

Down I-94 in Chicago, the Cubs had thumped the Cardinals, 8-4, at Wrigley Field, maintaining a one-game lead with two to play. Realizing how lucky the Brewers had been to escape with a victory against the Tigers, Counsell encouraged his players to focus on the task at hand and not worry about what Chicago was doing.

"It doesn't change anything for us," Counsell said. "Tomorrow is a big game. We've got a chance to take it down to the last day of the season with a win, no matter what."

The Brewers knew they would have some vital information when they took the field the next night. The Cubs and Cardinals were playing a Saturday afternoon game, and as the Brewers were taking batting practice later that day, the final went up on the scoreboard at Miller Park: St. Louis 2, Chicago 1.

With the incentive of knowing a victory would draw them even for first place, the Brewers nevertheless found themselves in another fight with the Tigers. But there was no slowing down Yelich, who might as well be wearing a Superman cape under his uniform. The now-obvious MVP knocked two more out of the park, including the decisive blow in the seventh inning, as Milwaukee repeated the 6-5 score of the previous evening.

Counsell and the rest of the team had run out of ways to describe what they were watching every night from Yelich, who like the mythical Roy Hobbs, seemingly could hit a home run whenever he wanted.

"We're sitting here every night and I say it's reached a new level, and then it reaches another level," Counsell said. "It's just special, man. To watch a player like this in a stretch like this, with the importance of the games for a team, is historical."

The Brewers were five games behind the Cubs entering their game on Labor Day at Miller Park, with 24 games to play. They still trailed by 2½ games with six games remaining. If both teams did the same thing on the final day of the season, win or lose, they would have a Game No. 163 showdown the next day at Wrigley Field. That venue was secured for Chicago by winning the season series, 11 games to 8, after jumping to an 8-1 start.

An identical drama was unfolding in the NL West, where the Los Angeles Dodgers and Colorado Rockies were tied for first place and also facing an extra game. So, 161 games had been played and two division titles still were up for grabs, along with the second Wild Card spot.

"To get it back within our control is huge," Travis Shaw said. "We don't have to look for help anymore. It's all on us right now. If we win out, we're going to win the division."

There would be no cliffhangers on the final day. Looking like a team that wanted to go home, the Tigers were thumped, 11-0, by the Brewers, who broke open the game with six runs in the seventh. At Wrigley, the Cardinals, officially eliminated from the Wild Card race the previous day, rolled over in a 10-5 romp by the Cubs.

As it turned out, 162 games would not be enough. The Brewers and Cubs finished with 95-67 records, best in the National League, setting up the one-game showdown that would count in the regular season standings.

How much was at stake? Practically, everything. The winner would claim the division crown and home-field advantage throughout the NL playoffs. The loser would host the Wild Card game the next night against the loser of yet another Game No. 163 between the Dodgers and Rockies in Los Angeles.

The Cubs, who survived a stretch of playing 30 days in a row, a gauntlet that ended in mid-September, had not blown their division lead as much as the Brewers erased it. Milwaukee went 19-7 in that final month, including seven consecutive victories to end the season.

Even one loss over that final week and Chicago would have repeated as NL Central champion.

"The big thing is, we earned this game," Counsell said. "We fought really hard to win this game. That's what feels good about it, and it gives us a shot at the division. You'd take that every single season."

Beyond playing the game at Wrigley, the Brewers would have to overcome another daunting obstacle. Somehow, some way, the Cubs managed to once again line up left-hander José Quintana to face Milwaukee, the team he owned. By altering his rotation in mid-September, Counsell lined up his best starter, Jhoulys Chacín, for a possible Wild Card game. Instead, he'd be pitching a day earlier, on short rest, in the biggest game of his life.

Chacín and Quintana matched up twice in September, with Quintana winning both games. The crafty lefty went 4-1 with a 2.17 ERA in six starts against the Brewers during the season, boosting his overall record against them to 5-2, 1.89 in eight starts since joining the Cubs.

"That doesn't surprise me," Braun said when told the Brewers would face Quintana again. "If I was them, that's the guy that makes the most sense. He's had so much success against us."

Even knowing they would face Quintana, the streaking Brewers were brimming with confidence, so much so that slugger Jesús Aguilar provided bulletin-board material for the Cubs without hesitation.

"They know they've got a problem tomorrow," Aguilar told reporters in the upbeat clubhouse, a proclamation that played to much ridicule on the Chicago airwaves.

The Brewers boarded buses and headed down the highway for Chicago. Everyone was in good spirits and optimistic about the next day. Players talked about how it was almost inevitable, not to mention fitting, to play the Cubs one more time. They knew it would be a hostile atmosphere the next afternoon but they were looking forward to the challenge.

The Brewers had gotten hot at exactly the right time. Why not make it eight in a row?

The teams had played low-scoring, pitcher-dominating games all season, so it was not surprising when No.

Ryan Braun reacts after hitting an RBI single during the eighth inning giving the Brewers a 3-1 lead in the deciding Game 163.
AP PHOTO

163 quickly settled into a duel between the starters. Quintana again proved a tough nut to crack, limiting the Brewers to one run over five innings, that coming on an RBI single by the unstoppable Yelich in the third. Chacín allowed only one hit over 5 2/3 innings, but that hit was a game-tying home run by Anthony Rizzo in the fifth.

It was still 1-1 in the top of the eighth when Orlando Arcia led off with a single, the third of his four hits in the game. Santana once again came through off the bench, batting for Knebel and delivering a double off lefty Justin Wilson. Side-arming righty Steve Cishek came on to face Lorenzo Cain, who foiled the move by lining a single to center, scoring Arcia to snap the tie.

Lefty Randy Rosario took over and struck out Yelich, a big out for the Cubs. Right-hander Brandon Kintzler came on to face Braun, who continued his late-season binge with another RBI hit to center, giving the Brewers a 3-1 lead. All they needed to do was record six more outs and the division title was theirs.

Counsell called on Hader, who uncharacteristically had been homer-prone over the past week, presumably to get through the eighth before yielding to Jeffress in the ninth. Hader returned to the form he flashed for most of the season, pitching a 1-2-3 inning with a pair of strikeouts, drawing the Brewers tantalizingly close to their first NL Central crown in seven years.

When the game moved to the bottom of the ninth, however, Jeffress did not trot in from the bullpen. Instead, Hader popped back out of the dugout and trotted to the mound, with rookie Brandon Woodruff warming in the pen. What was going on?

Reporters later were told that Jeffress was unavailable to pitch for undisclosed reasons. Counsell would not say what happened, and general manager David Stearns only said that Jeffress was OK and would be available for the postseason. Jeffress' absence would remain a mystery for some time until he eventually revealed he had an epileptic seizure that morning. Jeffress had played with epilepsy for many years but handled it with medication and never had been held out of action because of it.

Accustomed to pitching multiple innings, Hader struck out Daniel Murphy and retired Ben Zobrist on a fly to right before Javy Baéz singled to keep the Cubs alive and get Rizzo to the plate. In their memorable Labor Day confrontation at Miller Park, Rizzo had become the only left-handed hitter to go deep against Hader, making this moment even more compelling.

Rizzo did get good wood on a 1-2 fastball, sending it on an arc to deep right-center as Cubs fans roared and Brewers fans held their breath. But Keon Broxton, inserted as a defensive replacement in right field, settled under the ball in front of the warning track and squeezed it for the final out, touching off a mad dash to the mound and mob scene around Hader.

The tense 3-1 victory capped one of the greatest late-season surges in NL history, allowing the Brewers to wipe out a five-game deficit in 24 games. They won 28 of their final 38 games, including the last eight in a row, and needed every one to steal the title from the Cubs in their own yard.

The Brewers retired to the visiting clubhouse at Wrigley Field, so small that it more resembled a walk-in closet. The Cubs had been given a luxurious new home clubhouse as part of an ongoing renovation of that ancient edifice but visiting teams were left with cramped, out-of-date quarters that had players stumbling over top of each other while dressing for games.

Don't think the Brewers weren't looking forward to trashing the place. They had watched the Cubs exert their dominance in recent years, including a long-overdue World Series crown in 2016, and heard the roar of invading Chicago fans when the teams met in Milwaukee. Partying on their premises felt better than even they imagined.

Champagned flowed as if it were Niagara Falls in the cramped quarters. This was a celebration worthy of the improbable feat the Brewers had pulled off, against heavy odds.

Later, Braun would underline what it meant for the Brewers to party in both St. Louis and Chicago, beating teams that had kicked sand in their faces for years.

"They are two of the toughest places to win," he said. "Those teams have had so much success. We've seen them celebrate so many times. To have an opportunity to do it here was indicative of the success we've had and the challenge we met."

The players deserved credit for constantly pushing aside talk of the Wild Card race and insisting they could still win the division. They kept insisting even when they fell 3½ games behind on September 18, leaving only 10 games to play to make up that deficit. They never conceded, refusing to do so until mathematically eliminated, a day that never came.

"I give this group a tremendous amount of credit for not losing sight of the division," said Stearns, standing in a corner of the clubhouse, out of the line of fire from

Josh Hader dons the ski goggles in anticipation of the post-game celebration with his teammates following the Game 163 win over the Cubs.
AP PHOTO

popping corks. "Even when we were five games back, we could have said, 'Ok, we're just gunning for the wild card.' This group never thought that. It's pretty incredible we pulled it off."

The Brewers were well aware they might see the Cubs again later in the week. The winner of the Wild Card game between Chicago and Colorado Springs, which lost its Game No. 163 showdown with Los Angeles, would come to Milwaukee to open the NLDS. Were the Brewers and Cubs destined to meet yet again?

"There's a possibility we'll have to knock them off again," Counsell said. "That can wait for now. We'll enjoy this and celebrate what we've accomplished. It gives us a chance to exhale a little bit and let it sink in. We've been playing good baseball for quite a while."

The Cubs would not make it to Milwaukee, however. The next night, they bowed to the Rockies, 2-1, in a 13-inning marathon, ending their season. Such is the fragility of baseball. On Sunday, the Cubs were tied for first in the NL Central with the Brewers. On Tuesday night, they were packing to go home.

The Brewers would have two days to rest before taking on Colorado. They had earned it.

CHAPTER TWENTY ONE

Everybody loves free hamburgers

In 1987, when the Brewers got off to a blazing start to open the season, local restaurant chain George Webb announced it would live up to a promise made decades beforehand by its founder and give away free hamburgers. When the team reached that plateau on its surge to a 13-0 record, those restaurants indeed gave away burgers, reported to reach the astonishing level of 168,194 freebies, though people had to stand in line in the rain to get them.

At the time, George Webb promised it would hold the giveaway any time the team won 12 in a row, but years, then decades passed without the Brewers coming close. When the '18 Brewers clicked off eight victories in a row to close the season, including the Game No. 163 showdown in Chicago, rumblings began to circulate about another possible burger giveaway. Not shying away from the publicity, the restaurant vowed to do it again if the streak reached 12 games.

It seemed like a safe vow to make, even publicly. To get to 12 victories in a row, the Brewers would have to sweep Colorado in the best-of-five NLDS, then take Game 1 of the NLCS against a yet-to-be determined opponent. Nobody wins 12 in a row at that time of the year, when the best of the best are playing each other in the bubbling cauldron of October baseball.

With that foodie footnote filed away, the Brewers and Rockies prepared to open the NLCS at Miller Park. Colorado, which lost its Game 163 showdown in Los Angeles, had to survive the 13-inning Wild Card marathon in Chicago to advance, while Milwaukee's players held light workouts for a couple of days, getting some well-earned rest. The Brewers won the season

series between the clubs, five games to two, and
therefore felt confident about the matchup despite the
Rockies' power-packed lineup.

Counsell used the deep and talented bullpen to lead
the charge through the month of September, and wasn't
about to abandon that game plan. The day before Game
1, he said he would go with a "bullpen day" rather than
name a traditional starter. And Counsell did not reveal
which reliever would be first to pitch.

This is how the Brewers were going to play the
postseason. The tradition of naming your starting
pitchers for the first three games, allowing the other
team to align its batting order accordingly, was not for
them. If that was baseball etiquette, they decided to be
rude hosts. General manager David Stearns, Counsell
and their staffs broke down every possible way to attack
the Rockies, and decided this was best.

It wasn't as if the Brewers had no available starters
to select. Two pitchers who were in the season-ending
rotation, left-hander Wade Miley and righty Zach Davies,
were ready on full rest.

"We're going to use guys that haven't been our
starters this last couple weeks," Counsell said. "So,
we're going to use a bunch of different guys and we're
still deciding on exactly the order of that scenario."

No manager ran a game based more on pitcher/hitter
matchups than Counsell, and he was intent on keeping
the Rockies off-balance. He did announce that his top
starter, Jhoulys Chacín, would pitch Game 2 on short
rest, meaning he likely wouldn't go more than three
or four innings. Thus, that game would be primarily a
bullpen exercise as well.

Counsell used an "opener" in the final-week series in
St. Louis, having left-handed reliever Dan Jennings face
one batter, Matt Carpenter. Counsell said he wouldn't be
doing that against the Rockies, opting instead for two-
or three-inning appearances from a group of pitchers.

National pundits wondered aloud what the Brewers
were doing, but if they had paid close attention during
the season, especially the final month, they knew
Counsell went to his relief corps early and often.
Milwaukee's bullpen logged 614 innings, second-most in

the NL, and thrived under that heavy workload, posting a 3.47 ERA, second-best in the league.

Simply put, the relief corps had outperformed the starters. Chase Anderson, the Opening Day starter, had become so inconsistent with his mechanics, he was removed from the rotation with a week to go. As it would turn out, he had thrown his last pitch of the season. Davies was 0-2 with a 3.91 ERA in five starts in September but injuries limited him to 13 appearances for the season, and he was far from in peak form. Miley had been reliable when healthy but scuffled in his last two starts, allowing six earned runs in only seven innings.

Veteran lefty Gio Gonzalez, the August 31 pickup from Washington, performed well in his month with the club, going 3-0 with a 2.13 ERA in five starts, all of which the Brewers won. He would have been available on full rest for Game 2 but Counsell decided Chacín was his man.

The Brewers weren't trying to reinvent the wheel. They merely were trying to adjust the spokes to get it to run more efficiently. If it didn't work, they would hear about it, but Stearns and Counsell were far beyond worrying about such things. This is what they felt gave them the best chance to win, so conventional wisdom be damned. If it ruffled some feathers, too bad.

Counsell cautioned all season against the terms "starters" and "relievers," preferring to call his pitchers "out-getters." He also paid little attention to pitch counts, often pulling starters who had not been taxed because analytics suggested it was folly to allow them to face a lineup a third time. The Brewers had every reason to trust their bullpen, posting an 80-3 record when leading after seven innings.

"We just feel like with the pitchers we have available, they're going to share the 27 outs," Counsell explained. "We're going to share the outs a little bit more, but we really are confident with the days off in the series (after Games 2 and 4), the way we're coming into the series, that we'll be certainly able to do it."

Rockies manager Bud Black stuck with his regular starters, beginning with Antonio Senzatela in Game 1 and lefty Tyler Anderson in Game 2, with top starters

Kyle Freeland and Germán Marquez ready when the NLDS shifted to Coors Field.

Asked about the Brewers' unconventional approach to pitching in the series, including withholding the name of their Game 1 starter, Black refused to make a big deal about it, saying, "I think we'll adhere to Rule No. 1, which is be ready for anything."

The next day, it was revealed that young right-hander Brandon Woodruff would be the Brewers' first "outgetter" in Game 1. That choice surprised some, but it shouldn't have. A horse of a pitcher at 6-4, 232 pounds, Woodruff began the season in the starting rotation but did not last long before being sent to the minors, bouncing up and down six times.

His biggest impact would come as a September call-up, when Woodruff was added to the Brewers' deep and talented relief corps. He made seven appearances in that intense setting and prospered, posting a 0.73 ERA with 16 strikeouts in 12 1/3 innings. No longer having to pace himself as a starter, Woodruff could rear back and let the ball fly, and his velocity improved a few clicks into the high 90s (mph).

An 11th-round draft pick out of Mississippi State in 2014, Woodruff earned the organization's Pitcher of the Year Award in 2016, becoming something of a legend with an incredible display of mental toughness in late July at Class AA Biloxi. Woodruff's older brother, Blake, was killed in an ATV accident back home in Mississippi, and the shaken pitcher left the club to attend the funeral, with instructions to stay as long as he needed.

Instead, Woodruff returned to Biloxi after the funeral and insisted on pitching the next night against Pensacola. He tossed six shutout innings, and also hit his first professional home run, the only run in a 1-0 victory. Woodruff kept pushing, going 6-2 with a 2.02 ERA over his final nine starts.

With that background, Woodruff wasn't going to crack under the pressure of pitching in Game 1 of the NLDS. Sure enough, he went out and dominated the Rockies' lineup for three innings, allowing no hits before turning it over to the high-leverage relievers in the bullpen. Counsell didn't hesitate to follow Woodruff with another talented and competitive rookie, Corbin Burnes, who tossed two shutout innings.

Senzatela also showed up with his good stuff but was no match for the white-hot bat of Christian Yelich. At that point, who was? After a one-out walk by Lorenzo Cain in the third inning, Yelich sent a drive to left-center that cleared the fence for his first postseason home run, electrifying the home fans.

It would remain 2-0 as the Brewers went through a succession of their best bullpen arms until Counsell finally gave the ball in the ninth to Jeremy Jeffress, as planned. Jeffress was unavailable to close the division-clinching Game No. 163 in Chicago due to an epileptic seizure but was deemed good to go in the NLDS, and said beforehand he felt fine.

In what unfortunately for the Brewers would be a sign of things to come, Jeffress did not look fine. He found immediate trouble with singles by Gerardo Parra and Matt Holliday, bringing leadoff man Charlie Blackmon to the plate. Blackmon appeared to tie the game with a drive down the right-field line that umpire John Tumpane ruled fair, with both runners coming around as Blackmon raced to third.

The Brewers challenged the fair call on video replay, which showed the baseball struck a hair to the right of the foul line. Undaunted, Blackmon returned to the plate and singled to right, putting Colorado on the board and sending the tying run to second. What happened next was not Jeffress' fault. Shortstop Orlando Arcia muffed a slow roller by D.J. LeMahieu for an error that left the bases loaded.

Slugger Nolan Arenado fell behind in the count, 0-2, but drove a fly to deep center that scored the tying run. Blackmon was trapped off third base on David Dahl's grounder to first and tagged for a huge out, allowing Jeffress to escape without further damage by striking out Trevor Story.

Afterward, Jeffress tried to put a positive spin on the outing, saying, "I limited them to two runs, and it was good." But it would not be the last time he found trouble with games on the line.

The Brewers went down in order in the ninth against Adam Ottavino, and for the second time in club history, were headed to extra innings in the postseason. The first time worked out quite nicely – a clinching, 10-inning, 3-2 victory in Game 5 of the 2011 NLDS against Arizona, making Nyjer Morgan a cult hero in franchise lore for knocking in the winner. Seeking to channel that magic, the Brewers invited the excitable Morgan to throw out the ceremonial first pitch before the game.

Ottavino returned for the 10th inning and lost a seven-pitch battle to Yelich, who drew a walk, then advanced to second on a wild pitch. Ryan Braun went down swinging, prompting the Rockies to intentionally walk lefty-hitting Travis Shaw. Curtis Granderson grounded into a force at second, leaving it to Mike Moustakas, the veteran pickup in late July coveted in part for his postseason experience, including two World Series with Kansas City.

Moustakas fell behind in the count, 0-2, but refused to give in to Ottavino, the nastiest pitcher in the Rockies' bullpen. He fouled off the next pitch before lining a 96-mph fastball to right field for a single, scoring Yelich and giving the Brewers a walk-off victory that sent the crowd of 43,383 into a frenzy.

Always modest and a consummate team player, Moustakas declined to beat his chest afterward, saying, "Just got a good situation and was able to put the ball in play."

Of bouncing back from the Rockies' tying rally off Jeffress, Counsell said, "It feels good because that was a big punch, because of the way that we pitched the whole game. It's a punch that knocks you back a little bit, right? We took that blow and a bunch of guys kind of gutted through it."

Thanks to Moustakas channeling Morgan, who watched from the seats, the Brewers had won their ninth game in a row.

Counsell wasn't sure how far Chacín could go pitching on short rest for the second consecutive time in Game 2 but the de facto staff ace made things easier on his manager by pitching five scoreless innings, throwing 85 pitches. Once again, the bullpen would be counted on to cover nearly half the game, which again morphed into a pitchers' duel.

The Brewers finally broke through in the fourth against Anderson on a run-scoring double by Hernán Pérez, getting a rare start at shortstop. It stayed 1-0 until the eighth, when Moustakas struck again with an RBI single against Seunghwan Oh. Erik Kratz, the journeyman backup catcher finally getting his chance to play in October, made it 4-0 with a huge two-run single – a broken-bat blooper into shallow left that nevertheless was the biggest hit of his life.

Showing no reluctance whatsoever to go back to Jeffress after his Game 1 struggles, Counsell allowed him to cover the final two innings to seal the 4-0 victory. Afterward, Jeffress was in tears, trying to explain what it meant for his manager not to give up on him.

"The confidence that Counsell has in me, I can't put into words," said Jeffress, who held 4-year-old daughter Jurnee in his arms in the interview room. "I'm grateful."

The 10 consecutive victories tied for second-most in franchise history, the Brewers' longest streak since 2003. It was only the second postseason shutout for the Brewers and first since Game 1 of the 1982 World Series, when they thumped St. Louis, 10-0.

When the series shifted to Colorado, with the Rockies desperate to avoid a sweep, Counsell finally gave the ball to Miley, who made so many big starts down the stretch. He would go only 4 2/3 innings but by that point a short outing from the first "out-getter" seemed more like a plan than a problem.

Miley was followed by the usual high-leverage relievers, a fivesome that continued to keep Colorado off the board. The Brewers' offense made this one easy, with Jesús Aguilar, Arcia and Keon Broxton clouting home runs to lead the way to a 6-0 romp.

After jumping around on the field, the Brewers retreated to the visiting clubhouse for their third celebration in 12 days, all on the road. Before the champagne really got flowing, Braun gathered his teammates in a circle and delivered an impassioned speech, presenting the team's mission statement.

Relief pitcher Josh Hader jumps into the arms of catcher Erik Kratz after getting the Rockies Ian Desmond for the final out of Game 3 of the National League Division Series.
AP PHOTO

"Two weeks ago in St. Louis, we came out with a goal," Braun shouted to the group. "The goal was to win the World Series. We've taken steps in that direction. Two weeks ago in St. Louis, we said, 'Let's make this the first celebration and not the last.' Two celebrations later, we've got two celebrations to go.

"We accomplished this by everybody playing to the best of their abilities. Everybody here is doing their job the best they possibly can. That's why we're winning baseball games. Nothing's going to change. The lights are going to get brighter. It's going to be more fun than we've had to this point. We will keep doing the same shit!"

The team that supposedly did not have enough starting pitching, with too much reliance on the bullpen, had dominated the Rockies so thoroughly, it was difficult to digest. Colorado scored in only one of the 28 innings played, for a total of two runs, the lowest output in NLDS history. The Brewers blanked the Rockies over the final 19 innings. The initial "out-getters" – don't say the word "starters" – did not allow a run in 12 2/3 innings.

The Rockies finished with a mere 14 hits, batting .146 as a team with a .188 slugging percentage, if you could call it that. Milwaukee's pitchers posted a 0.64 ERA in the three games, with 30 strikeouts over those 28 innings.

The joke was on the rest of the baseball world. The Brewers did have enough pitching. And don't dare fall behind before the door to the bullpen swings open. The overpowering relief corps would put you to bed without dinner.

"We've pitched at a really high level for some time," Counsell said. "To give up two runs in three games, and finish it with a shutout here, in the most difficult place to pitch in baseball, those guys deserve a ton of credit."

The Brewers had won 11 games in a row, an unfathomable streak at this stage of a season. Hungry fans across Milwaukee could practically smell George Webb cooking up those free hamburgers.

CHAPTER TWENTY TWO

One victory short

The Dodgers also rolled through their NLDS against Atlanta, though they did lose once, bowing 6-5 in Game 3. Their first two victories were shutouts, and the Brewers knew they would be challenged by Los Angeles' vaunted pitching staff, led by ace Clayton Kershaw, the Game 1 starter for the NLCS.

"To me, he's the greatest pitcher of our generation, and on the short list of greatest pitchers of all time," Ryan Braun said as the Brewers prepared for the Friday afternoon opener at Miller Park.

In terms of market size and financial resources, the NLCS was a David and Goliath matchup. The Dodgers opened the season with a payroll of some $187 million, more than twice the Brewers' salary total of about $91 million. Advancing this far was old hat for Los Angeles, playing in its third NLCS and fourth in six years. Milwaukee hadn't been in this baseball stratosphere since 2011.

Once again, manager Craig Counsell waited to announce his pitching plans, mulling the various ways he could attack the Dodgers' lineup combinations while keeping counterpart Dave Roberts guessing. On the day before the opener, he revealed his first three starters, and while the names were not unexpected, the order was a bit of a surprise.

Lefties Gio Gonzalez and Wade Miley would start the first two games, with the Brewers' most dependable pitcher, Jhoulys Chacín, set for Game 3 in Los Angeles. Chacín's assignment was interesting because the last time he pitched in Dodger Stadium, on Aug. 2, he was

Brewers pitcher Brandon Woodruff (53) celebrates after crushing a home run off of Dodgers ace Clayton Kershaw during the third inning of Game 1 of the National League Championship Series.
AP PHOTO

pummeled for nine runs, including three homers, in a 21-5 shellacking.

"That was my toughest game of the season," Chacín admitted. "It's going to be a big challenge but it's also going to be fun to have (a chance for) redemption there."

As usual, Counsell threw some doubt into the equation by saying he wouldn't hesitate to use Chacín in Game 1 if necessary, which would eliminate him from the Game 3 assignment. So, the chess match continued.

As it turned out, Counsell asked only two innings of Gonzalez, who surrendered a leadoff home run to Manny Machado in the second. Brandon Woodruff, the starting pitcher turned late-season reliever, again would get thrust into the fray as the Brewers challenged yet another opponent to beat their bullpen.

The unexpected often happens in the postseason but what took place in the bottom of the third inning was both shocking and wonderful, at the same time. Seeking to get another inning out of Woodruff, Counsell allowed him to bat against Kershaw. A right-handed pitcher who batted from the left side, Woodruff got all of a 2-2 fastball and crushed it off the corner of the scoreboard in center, tying the game and electrifying the crowd.

As astonished as everyone else at what just happened, Woodruff let out a roar as he rounded first base, turning to look back at the Brewers' dugout with a massive grin on his face. Kershaw would not be the same after that blast – only the fourth homer ever by a pitcher off him – and exited in the fifth as Milwaukee bolted to a 5-1 lead.

"It certainly changed the energy in our dugout from what you think is going to be a kind of grind-it-out game against Clayton," Counsell said. "When that happens, it gives everybody life. It definitely changed the vibe."

The modest, soft-spoken Woodruff declined to boast afterward about his stunning feat, so his teammates did it for him.

"He should be able to talk about that the rest of his life," Brewers third baseman Mike Moustakas said. "He's a legend in Milwaukee right now."

With a 6-1 lead entering the eighth and the game in the hands of their superior relief corps, the Brewers appeared headed for a cruise-control victory. But the

Dodgers had other ideas, loading the bases with one out against Xavier Cedeño and Rafael Soria. As he had done many times during the season in such jams, Counsell summoned Jeffress, in search of an escape act.

But this wasn't the same Jeffress. His postseason slide continued as Machado singled in two runs and Matt Kemp singled in another. Jeffress finally ended the inning by striking out Yasiel Puig but it now was 6-4 and anything but a done deal for the Brewers.

Corey Knebel, as close to a sure thing as Counsell had in his bullpen since the start of September, made the home crowd nervous in the ninth by issuing a two-out walk to Joc Pederson and RBI triple to Chris Taylor, making it a one-run game. Knebel recovered to strike out the dangerous Justin Turner, ending a six-pitch duel with a high 97-mph fastball and allowing the Brewers to finally exhale with a hard-fought victory.

The Brewers had won 12 in a row, and for the first time since 1987, the local George Webb restaurant chain would live up to a promise made by its founder so long ago. Those with a hankering for a free hamburger would get one on October 18, at any of its 30 locations. Limited to a four-hour window that day, nearly 100,000 were served.

Before the game, Counsell had joked, "Who knew that we would make it this far and the biggest piece of stress going into this game would be George Webb's hamburgers?"

The Dodgers weren't done chipping away at the Brewers' previously indomitable bullpen. With a 3-0 lead entering the seventh inning of Game 2, Milwaukee appeared poised to take a commanding two-game advantage in the NLCS. Miley had come through in grand fashion in the biggest start of his career, blanking Los Angeles on two hits over 5 2/3 innings.

Rookie Corbin Burnes, who dominated Colorado in the NLDS with four scoreless innings, didn't retire any of the three hitters he faced in the seventh, getting chased by Cody Bellinger's RBI single. Counsell, who had used strikeout sensation Josh Hader for three scoreless innings in Game 1, had little choice but to give Jeffress another chance to get his postseason on track.

After a jam-shot single by Pederson loaded the
bases, Jeffress gave himself a chance to stop it there
by striking out Puig. Instead, he issued a walk to light-
hitting backup catcher Austin Barnes, forcing in a run
that cut Milwaukee's lead to 3-2. Jeffress recovered
to get Yasmani Grandal to bounce into a double play,
keeping the Brewers on top, now by a mere run.

Jeffress, who hadn't been quite the same since his
seizure in Chicago before Game No. 163, was being
tormented by a frustrating combination of bad luck and
bad pitches. Many of the hits he surrendered in the
postseason were not struck well but still found holes,
keeping innings alive and opening the door for him to
make mistakes, particularly when pitching behind in the
count.

That trend continued in the eighth when Taylor led
off with a tapper toward third base that went for an
infield hit, much to the dismay of Jeffress. When he
fell behind in the count to Turner, 2-0, Jeffress had to
throw one over the plate and the Dodgers third baseman
did not miss it, sending it out to left on a line, giving Los
Angeles a 4-3 lead that quieted the packed house.

With the potential tying run on second in the bottom
of the ninth, Dodgers closer Kenley Jansen induced
Christian Yelich to tap out to third, sending the home
crowd home in disappointment. Instead of taking a 2-0
lead in the series to Los Angeles, the Brewers had to
settle for a split. In doing so, the air of invincibility of
their bullpen was slipping away, giving the Dodgers'
hitters confidence that few opponents had enjoyed.

"You can't take anything away from that pen," Roberts
said. "They've done it over the course of the season, and
they're a tough pen to match up against. But we talked
about seeing those guys two nights in a row. I think that
plays to our advantage."

How tough was the loss to take for the Brewers?
During the regular season, Milwaukee had won 80 of 83
games when taking a lead into the eighth. It was obvious
afterward that Jeffress had no answers for why his
regular-season brilliance faded in October.

"They hit a home run, something that's left up," he
said in a quiet home clubhouse. "You can't take nothing

away from those guys over there. They're professionals like everybody else. Just make a pitch. That's all I've got to do."

Jeffress rarely had such moments in the regular season, when he went 8-1 with a 1.29 ERA and 15 saves in 73 appearances, holding opponents to a .182 batting average. Turner's homer was the 11th hit Jeffress allowed in the postseason in 4 2/3 innings while compiling a 7.73 ERA.

The Brewers' pitching plan actually was thrown out of whack when Burnes couldn't get an out in the seventh, prompting some second-guessers to suggest Counsell should have left Miley in the game. But this was how Counsell had run the bullpen all season, in particular the final month, with tremendous results. Nobody crunched the numbers more than the Brewers, and analytics showed most pitchers struggled the third time through a lineup.

That strategy didn't work this time. But, right or wrong, Counsell would not give up on Jeffress. That wasn't his style. The wiry manager could be stubbornly loyal to his players, allowing them to fail for longer periods than fans understood, but that's why they played so hard for him, why they never gave up on him. They appreciated that loyalty and his emphasis on "staying connected" at all times.

All season long, the Brewers counted on Chacín in big games, and for the most part, he had delivered. He did so in Game No. 163 in Chicago. He did it again in Game 2 of the NLDS against Colorado. Chacín rarely pitched in truly big games in his previous five stops in the majors, with no appearances in the postseason.

But the soft-spoken veteran always believed, if given the chance, he could succeed under pressure. He wasn't a hard thrower but had tremendous fastball command and knew how to spin a baseball, which attracted the Brewers in the first place. Chacín had learned to throw a decent changeup, and wasn't above quick-pitching a hitter every now and then, much to their frustration.

Matched up against sensational Dodgers rookie Walker Buehler, Chacín delivered once again with 5 1/3 shutout innings, allowing only three hits and two walks, with six strikeouts. The way he was throwing the ball, the Brewers weren't going to need a ton of offense but Braun got things started immediately with an RBI double in the first that followed a one-out walk by Yelich.

It stayed 1-0 until the sixth when Buehler helped the Brewers' cause with a run-scoring wild pitch after Travis Shaw's booming two-out triple to center. That lead doubled to 4-0 the next inning when Erik Kratz doubled down the left-field line with one down and Orlando Arcia followed with an opposite-field drive to right that carried out for his second homer of the postseason. This was not the same Arcia who struggled so badly during the regular season he was demoted to the minors twice.

With a 4-0 lead at that late stage, it should have been a cruise-control victory for the Brewers, particularly with the machine-like manner in which their bullpen usually finished off opponents. But, instead of giving the final inning to Hader, who struck out both hitters he faced in the eighth, Counsell once again summoned the struggling Jeffress.

While puzzling on the surface, there was a method to Counsell's madness. He figured he'd need Jeffress again if the Brewers were going to win the NLCS, and thought a four-run cushion would allow him to relax a little and regroup on the mound. Instead, Jeffress threw a scare into Counsell and everyone in the traveling party.

Following recent alarming patterns, Jeffress found immediate trouble. Turner, who beat him with the eighth-inning home run in Game 2, led off with a single and raced to third on Machado's double to left. Jeffress recovered briefly by popping up Bellinger but Puig drew a walk to load the bases, bringing to the plate Grandal, a dangerous hitter with considerable left-handed power.

Much to the dismay of the Brewers and their fans, including those back home watching on TV, the Dodgers had the tying run at the plate, and a home-run hitter at that, with only one out. Perched on the top step of the dugout, Counsell did not make a move to the mound. Jeffress rewarded that confidence by striking out Grandal on three pitches, then catching pinch-hitter

Brian Dozier looking at a 97-mph fastball to end the game.

Whew!

Afterward, Counsell would act as if he had no doubt in the outcome, saying, "We got a four-run lead. I trust (Jeffress) to get those outs. The ninth inning was entertaining but they didn't score."

As for pulling Hader after striking out two hitters, Counsell said, "We're trying to win the series. We're not just trying to win games here. We're trying to win the series. We put ourselves in Games 4 and 5 with tonight's effort."

But Game 4 would deplete the pitching staffs on both sides. That's what happens when you have to cover 13 innings, with games before and afterward in a postseason series. It would prove to be a long night in particular for the Brewers, in more ways than one.

The game couldn't have gotten off to a worse start for the Brewers on the pitching front, considering how many innings would be played. Puig opened the bottom of the second with a high comebacker to the mound that Gonzalez leaped to try to grab, only to land awkwardly and roll his left ankle. After being attended to for several minutes, Gonzalez said he wanted to stay but after throwing just one pitch had to leave in pain. As it turned out, his season was done.

The Dodgers had taken a 1-0 lead off Gonzalez in the first on Dozier's two-out, run-scoring single, and Los Angeles starter Rich Hill made it hold up until the fifth. With one down, Arcia reached on an infield hit and Domingo Santana continued his uncanny success off the bench with a booming double to right-center that tied the game.

At that point, the pitchers took over the game completely, putting the respective offenses into a deep freeze. Freddy Peralta, who hadn't pitched since September 24, came on to pitch three brilliant, hitless innings for the Brewers, with six strikeouts. Burnes followed with two more scoreless innings, also allowing no hits. That stretch provided an exciting look into the future of pitching in Milwaukee, featuring two arms expected to make an impact in Peralta and Burnes.

Both managers dug deep into their bullpens as the hitters continued to snooze. There finally was some action in the bottom of the 10th inning but it had more to do with poor sportsmanship than offense. On what should have been a routine groundout, Machado appeared to intentionally stick out his left leg as he got to the bag, clipping the back leg of first baseman Jesús Aguilar.

Aguilar, who was fortunate not to suffer an injury, was understandably miffed, and let Machado know it. The two exchanged words, leading to both dugouts and bullpens emptying onto the field before calmer heads ruled. Aguilar later showed forgiveness for Machado, saying they had made peace, but his Brewers teammates were not as charitable, basically calling him a punk. Never mind that Milwaukee had tried hard to acquire Machado before the trade deadline, only to be outbid by the Dodgers.

Machado already had drawn the ire of the Brewers with two rough slides into second base in Game 3, grabbing for Arcia's legs both times to try to thwart throws to first. He was called for obstruction on one after video review, resulting in a double play being awarded to Milwaukee.

"It was a dirty play by a dirty player," said Yelich, never one to pop off without good reason. "He is a player who has a history with those types of incidents. One time is an accident. Repeated, over and over again, it's a dirty play.

"I have a lot of respect for him as a player but you can't respect someone who plays the game like that. Run through the bag like you've done your whole life, like everybody else does."

Strong words from the presumptive NL MVP. The normally understated Counsell also would land a verbal punch to the chin of Machado. Asked if he thought the slides at second base the previous night and the play at first base were an indication of Machado playing the game hard, the irked manager said, "I don't think he's playing all that hard."

Counsell summoned former starter Junior Guerra to pitch that inning, telling him he likely had the rest of the game, within reason. Guerra responded brilliantly to that challenge, putting the side down in order for three consecutive innings and stretching it to 10 hitters retired until Machado lined a single to left with one down in the 13th.

Machado advanced to second with two down on a wild pitch, which proved huge when Bellinger lined a 3-2 fastball from Guerra to right field for an RBI single that finally ended the 5-hour, 15-minute marathon. Afterward, Counsell would have to answer for why the Brewers pitched to Bellinger when they could have walked him and the next hitter, Grandal, to load the bases and get to pitcher Julio Urias, with no hitters remaining on the Dodgers bench.

"We were trying to expand (the strike zone) on Cody Bellinger," Counsell explained. "We just left a pitch too much up to Bellinger. I thought it was worth the risk to try to expand to Bellinger, and then if he walks, we walk Grandal and pitch to Urias. Once we had two strikes, we just got too much of the plate."

In other words, Counsell left it to Guerra, likely a bit fatigued after throwing 50 pitches, and he failed to execute the plan. A manager runs that risk anytime he leaves it to the players in such situations. To say the least, it was a crushing loss for the Brewers, who instead of holding a commanding 3-1 lead, allowed the Dodgers to draw even with one more game at home.

You certainly couldn't hang this one on the Brewers' pitching staff, which compiled a franchise-record 17 strikeouts in a postseason game. Even with Gonzalez's unexpected early exit, Milwaukee's pitchers tossed 11 consecutive scoreless innings after the first, which should have been good enough to emerge victorious.

"It hurts where your pitchers go out there and keep those guys at one run for 12 innings," said leadoff hitter Lorenzo Cain, who went 0 for 6 with three strikeouts. "You want to win that game. We've got to turn this thing around and score some more runs for those guys because they've just been so good for us all season long."

In what turned out to be a cruel bit of scheduling, the teams had to sleep quick and get back out to Dodger

Stadium for Game 5, an afternoon contest. Even worse for the Brewers, it again was Kershaw's turn to pitch, and he wasn't likely to deliver a second consecutive subpar outing following his Game 1 loss.

Counsell would have one more pitching trick up his sleeve. He announced the left-handed Miley would start the game but it would turn out to be another "opener" move, and not an effective one. Miley would face only one batter, the lefty-hitting Bellinger, who drew a walk, before yielding to young buck Woodruff, the pitcher expected to carry the early load that day.

The Brewers' pitching maneuverings were not the story of this game, however. Their offense would not recover from being placed in the deep freeze the previous evening, scratching out only five hits. After Milwaukee took a 1-0 lead in the third on an RBI double by Cain, and Braun drew a two-out walk, Kershaw and three relievers combined to retire 18 consecutive batters before Aguilar and Curtis Grandson doubled in consecutive at-bats in the ninth.

The 5-2 final put the Brewers one loss from elimination, an ugly turn of events after they blanked the Dodgers in Game 3. Los Angeles' pitchers had something to say about that turnabout but the Brewers knew the offense had let the team down, particularly in the Game 4 marathon. They scored a mere three runs over the last 22 innings in LA, which wasn't going to cut it.

In particular, the Dodgers had neutralized Yelich, who lifted his team and carried it into October baseball with his MVP-clinching offensive binge. They were constantly pounding him up and in, and he wasn't getting many good swings. He also looked a touch weary after going so hard for so long, doing so much.

"He's just not on right now," Counsell said of Yelich, who was 3-for-20 (.150), all singles, with no RBI, four walks and five strikeouts. "I'm glad we're going back home."

Not that Yelich was the Brewers' only no-show at the plate. Mike Moustakas, the late-season pickup coveted for his postseason experience in Kansas City, was in a 2-for-21 slide (.095). Aguilar's average in the series had

Orlando Arcia celebrates his home run with third base coach Ed Sedar during the fifth inning of Game 2 of the National League Championship Series.

AP PHOTO

dropped to .222. Braun was actually one of the "hotter" hitters at .238, an indication of how bad things were going for Milwaukee's offense.

"One run here, two runs there, that's not going to cut it against the Dodgers, I can tell you that," Cain said. "Hopefully, we'll go home and regroup. At the end of the day, we've got to find a way to get it done."

The Brewers still felt confident about their pitching heading back to Milwaukee. Part of the "opening" plan with Miley was to start him for a second consecutive time in Game 6, but for more than one batter this time. That would leave the Brewers with their ace, Chacín, on full rest for Game 7. All they needed was for the offense to emerge from its hibernation.

There was no panic among the ranks of the Brewers. The way they saw it, they merely needed a two-game winning streak at Miller Park, where they went 51-30 during the regular season. Raucous, jam-packed home crowds had energized them for weeks when it mattered most, and they'd count on that noisy backing again.

To recapture some momentum in the series, not to mention staying alive another day, the Brewers needed something good to happen early in Game 6. There was a slight hiccup in the top of the first when longtime Brewers killer David Freese led off the game with a home run off Miley but that would soon be forgotten by a Milwaukee crowd looking for something to cheer.

Dodgers starter Hyun-Jin Ryu was in position to escape the bottom of the inning with no damage when Aguilar stepped to the plate with two on and two down but the offensive dam finally broke for the Brewers. Aguilar lined a double to right, scoring two runs. Moustakas also doubled to right, knocking in Aguilar. Kratz, the journeyman catcher who made such a difference over the second half of the season after being acquired from the Yankees, kept the volume turned up in the stands with an RBI single that made it 4-1.

How big was that four-run rally? It represented more runs than the Brewers scored in the previous two games in Los Angeles, covering 22 innings. And they weren't done. The next inning, Yelich snapped out of his postseason skid with a one-out double off Ryu and trotted around when Braun followed with another two-bagger.

"Especially after they jumped ahead on David Freese's homer, I thought it would be incredibly important for us to answer back as quickly as possible," Braun said. "Keep the crowd in it. Keep the pressure off us. It was inspiring for us the rest of the game."

Miley protected the 5-1 lead into the fifth, when Freese struck yet again with a run-scoring double. When Max Muncy followed with a walk, that was enough for Counsell, who summoned Knebel, the ninth-inning specialist at the start of the season who was injured and later lost that job, only to bounce back better than ever in September.

This was no time to mess around, with elimination looming, and Knebel got the job done, retiring Turner on a fly to deep right-center and striking out Machado, an inning-ender that drove the crowd into a frenzy. After Machado's dirty deeds in LA, Milwaukee's fans greeted him from the outset with booing of epic proportions, a deafening reception that even stunned the Brewers' players.

That would be the last wimper by the Dodgers as the Brewers cruised to a 7-2 victory, evening the series. A notable turn of events came in the seventh when Jeffress, given a three-run lead, breezed through a 1-2-3 inning before turning it over to Burnes, who put down the final six hitters in order. Counsell wanted so much to get Jeffress going, and hoped this would be the outing that did it.

The Brewers had assured a Game 7, their first since losing the 1982 World Series to the St. Louis Cardinals. With the offense finally awakened, anything seemed possible. A win would put them into their long-awaited second Fall Classic against the powerhouse Boston Red Sox, who had thumped defending champion Houston in five games in the ALCS.

"Playing a Game 7 means the world," Braun said in an upbeat home clubhouse. "It's exciting for me. It's exciting for everybody in our organization. It's exciting for our fans. I'm sure the energy and the enthusiasm in the ballpark tomorrow will be unlike anything any of us have experienced here."

Considering how dire their situation looked leaving LA, the Brewers were set up nicely to make it to the World Series. Their best starter, Chacín, was fully rested and coming off a Game 3 gem in which he blanked the Dodgers for 5 1/3 innings. Beyond that, Counsell did not have to use his most dominant reliever, Hader, who therefore would be available for multiple innings in the finale if needed.

If the Brewers were looking for another early omen as Game 7 began, they got one. With one down in the bottom of the first, Yelich – who had been stymied so effectively by the Dodgers' staff – drove a 98-mph fastball from Buehler out to right-center for his first home run and RBI of the NLCS. Just like that, the home crowd was in full throat, ready for another celebration and the first at home after three on the road.

There was no way to know as Yelich circled the bases that the rest of the game would be a dud for the Brewers. Buehler silenced their offense before departing in the fifth, turning it over to the Dodgers' strong bullpen. Chacín, on the other hand, would have a short night, exiting after two innings. Bellinger had struck again in the second with a two-run homer, and Counsell decided it best to get Hader in the game.

"You're looking at the game as a nine-inning season, and we were losing the game at that point," Counsell explained later. "So, we had to go with our best guy."

Before Bellinger's homer, Machado answered the cascade of boos from the home crowd with a daring bunt hit on a 3-2 count. Chacín thought he caught him off-guard by quick-pitching him but Machado had an answer.

"Perfect bunt," Chacín said. "I was surprised."

Once again, Hader would be brilliant, pitching three shutout innings with four strikeouts. After he was done in the top of the fifth, the game turned for good against the Brewers on a defensive gem from an unexpected source. A two-out double by Cain knocked Buehler out of the game, with Roberts summoning Urias, a lefty, to face Yelich.

It appeared Yelich had foiled that strategy when he sent an opposite-field drive to deep left but Taylor, who played all over the field for the Dodgers as needed during the season, raced back and hauled it in on the run as he reached the warning track, stretching his glove hand as far as he could before sliding to a stop.

"First glance, I didn't think he was going to catch it," Counsell said. "He covered a ton of ground. That was what was so impressive, the ground he covered."

As deflating as that play was, the air completely came out of Miller Park in the next inning. Again, it was the struggling Jeffress who paid the price. Coming in with a runner on and no outs, Jeffress allowed a single by his nemesis, Turner, but retired Machado on a fly to right and induced Bellinger to ground into a force.

Puig, who had been shut down for the most part in the first six games, got all of a 1-1 fastball from Jeffress and crushed it way out to center for a three-run home run, the proverbial dagger. Animated as always, Puig virtually moon-walked around the bases, gesturing wildly as the crowd sat in stunned silence.

Jeffress had run out of explanations for his postseason woes, merely saying later, "That's baseball. For me, that at-bat, the whole series, I've been throwing good pitches. I've just been getting hit."

The Brewers went quietly after that blow. Jansen, who never had allowed them a run during his career, pitched a scoreless eighth. The Dodgers then rubbed it in by giving Kershaw the ninth, a bit of Hollywood theatrics that ended Milwaukee's season.

An emotional Counsell gathered his players in the somber clubhouse afterward and told them they had the right to be disappointed but not to be despondent.

"You took us on an amazing journey," he told them, tears in his eyes. "You really did. It was an incredible journey that we should all be grateful for being part of because it was a magical run."

National pundits figured it would be the Brewers' pitching that betrayed them against the Dodgers but it did not play out that way. Other than Jeffress' struggles out of the pen, the real issue was an offense that scored only seven runs in the four losses, including one in the 13-inning loss in Game 4.

"The bottom line was they pitched better than we did," Counsell said. "They didn't let us get anything going in those games. Give them credit."

The Brewers finished with 102 victories, most in franchise history in one year. Hard to argue with that level of success but 103 would have put them on the game's grandest stage.

"We would have liked to take that last step," Yelich said, after his season for the ages finally came to an end. "We were one game away from the World Series. We can be proud of what we did. We played amazing down the stretch. We had to win a lot of tough games and tough series to give ourselves this opportunity."

From teardown in 2015 to one game shy of the World Series in 2018. The Brewers had arrived ahead of schedule.

EPILOGUE

Only one team gets to win its final game of the season. That honor went to the Boston Red Sox, who finished one of the most successful seasons in Major League history by throttling the Dodgers, four games to one, in the World Series.

Had the Brewers knocked off the Dodgers, they probably would have suffered the same fate at the hands of the mighty Red Sox. But they sure would have liked the honor of trying to avoid that fate.

Though it might have seemed that way, the Brewers didn't lose the NLCS in Game 7. They lost it by blowing a late lead in Game 2, and again in Game 4 by scoring only one run in 13 innings. But the Dodgers had something to say about it, doing what was necessary to win both games.

So, the wait for another World Series continued. And it hurt to come that close and fail. No matter how strong a team is, there are no guarantees of advancing that far through the layers of postseason play. The Brewers won 12 games in a row just to get to Game 2 of the NLCS.

As the pain dimmed in the succeeding weeks, the Brewers and their fans realized just how special this group was, and how for weeks on end they were the talk of the baseball world. Timing in life is everything, and the Brewers caught fire at exactly the right time, making up the five-game deficit to the Cubs they faced on Labor Day.

Brewers fans will long cherish the Game No. 163 victory at Wrigley Field, stealing the NL Central away from the Cubs in their own yard. In the history of the franchise, few victories have tasted as sweet. Everything

A young fan holds a sign that sums up what many Milwaukee Brewers fans felt in 2018.
AP PHOTO

after that was gravy on the cake, to quote the late, great George "Boomer" Scott.

There was no way to see this coming when the Brewers began their rebuilding process three years earlier, which is what made the season truly special and memorable. Few "experts" gave them any chance to knock off the Dodgers, yet the NLCS came down to a winner-take-all Game 7.

Before the Brewers were done, the city of Milwaukee got free hamburgers, almost always a good thing. But that was merely a fun footnote. The real story in October was what was happening in Miller Park, which was as electric as it ever has been. That was the place to be, and those who managed to get tickets had the time of their lives.

In the end, that's all you can really ask. Nothing else is promised. As manager Craig Counsell advised fans many times in those final weeks, hop on and enjoy the ride.